ADOLF HITLER'S
ZWEITES BUCH

BUCH
GERMAN FOREIGN POLICY

Cover art, visual design, and logos copyrighted by© 2024 Friendly Father

Book layout, design, and translation copyrighted by © 2024 Daniel Zakal

Published by © 2024 Invisible Empire Publishing

Hardcover ISBN: 978-1-963591-09-5

Printed in the United States of America

Trigger/Offensive Content Warning and General Disclaimer:

CONTENTS

CONTENTS

———————————————— 19 ————————————————

PUBLISHER'S FORWARD

———————————————— 28 ————————————————

Imagine uncovering a hidden chapter from one of history's most infamous figures. In 1928, a mysterious manuscript emerged, penned by Adolf Hitler himself, but it remained unpublished, locked away from the world's eyes. This enigmatic work, initially titled "Deutsche Aussenpolitik" and later known as Hitler's "Second Book," was dedicated to his close ally, Max Annan, the head of the National Socialist Party's publishing powerhouse. Today, you hold the key to this long-concealed document, offering an unprecedented look into the unfiltered mind of the Fuhrer.

Contrary to popular belief, it wasn't the lukewarm reception of Mein Kampf that kept this manuscript in the shadows. Instead, it was the relentless whirlwind of political chaos and Hitler's rapid ascent to power that relegated the manuscript to the depths of obscurity. As the National Socialist Party navigated through a maze of national elections and political upheavals, the manuscript lay forgotten, its raw contents unpolished and unrefined.

In a dramatic twist of fate, the manuscript resurfaced from the ashes of history. In the winter of 1950–51, two astute military intelligence linguists, sifting through mountains of German records, stumbled upon what appeared to be a mere draft of Mein Kampf. Little did they know, they had unearthed a lost treasure. This manuscript, which had narrowly escaped destruction in the final days of the war, lay dormant until a German historian's inquisitive mind sparked its rediscovery.

This edition is more than just a translation; it's a thrilling expedition into the depths of history. We've painstakingly restored and translated Hitler's unadulterated thoughts in English. Prepare as you delve into the pages of Hitler's lost manuscript, a document that offers a rare window into the National Socialist ideology and ambitions of one of the most controversial leaders in history. This is not just a book; it's a journey into the heart of National Socialist ideology on Foreign Policy.

---- 19 ----

ADOLF HITLER'S PREFACE

---- 28 ----

In August 1925, during the writing of the second volume, I briefly outlined the fundamental ideas of a National Socialist German foreign policy, as circumstances required. Within the scope of this work, I particularly addressed the South Tyrolean issue, which served as the pretext for as vehement as unjustified attacks against the movement. In 1926, I found it necessary to publish this section of the second volume as a separate edition.

I did not believe that this would convert those opponents who saw the agitation against South Tyrol as a desired means of combating the detested National Socialist movement as a whole. These people cannot be enlightened because for them, the question of truth or error, right or wrong, does not play any role. As soon as a matter seems suitable for their partly partisan, partly even highly personal interests, the truthfulness or correctness of such a matter is completely disregarded by these individuals.

This is even more the case when it can undermine a general uprising of our people. For the men who sought the destruction of Germany during the collapse are its current rulers, and their mindset from that time has not changed to this day. Just as they callously sacrificed Germany then for the sake of party doctrines or personal advantages, so do they hate anyone today who opposes their interests, even if they may have a thousand reasons for

German resurgence on their side. Indeed, even more so.

As soon as they believe they see a revival of our people represented by a particular name, they tend to oppose everything that could emanate from such a name. The most useful suggestions, indeed self-evident suggestions, are then boycotted simply because their bearer appears to be associated with general ideas that they feel compelled to combat from their partisan and personal perspective. Trying to convert such people is [impossible] hopeless.

Therefore, when I published my then South Tyrolean brochure in 1926, I naturally did not believe for a second that I could make an impression on those who already, due to their general ideological and political orientation, viewed me as the fiercest enemy. However, at that time, I hoped that at least some of the opponents of our National Socialist foreign policy, who were not inherently malicious, would examine our views on this matter and then judge accordingly. This undoubtedly happened in numerous cases.

Today, I can point out with satisfaction that a very large number of men, also active in public political life, have revised their previous stance on German foreign policy. And even if they did not believe they could adopt our standpoint in every detail, they have nevertheless acknowledged the honorable intentions guiding us. However, over the past two years, it has become increasingly clear to me that my former writing was actually based on generally accepted National Socialist insights as a prerequisite.

Many did not follow, not so much out of ill will as out of a certain inability. At that time, it was not possible to provide a truly fundamental argument within the narrow confines for the correctness of our National Socialist foreign policy views. Today, I feel compelled to rectify this.

For the attacks of the opponents have not only intensified in recent years but they have also mobilized the large camp of the indifferent to a certain extent. The agitation systematically waged against Italy for the past five years is gradually threatening to bear fruit, which could lead to the death and destruction of the last hopes of a German resurrection. As often seen in other matters, today the National Socialist movement stands completely isolated and solitary in its foreign policy stance within the German people and its political life. Alongside the attacks from the general enemies of our people and homeland from within, we encounter the proverbial stupidity and incompetence of the bourgeois-national parties, the indolence of the broad masses, and, as a particularly powerful ally, cowardice. This cowardice, which we can observe today in all those who are fundamentally incapable of resisting the Marxist plague and who, for this reason, consider themselves fortunate to lend their voice to public opinion on a matter less dangerous than the fight against Marxism, yet appearing and sounding somewhat similar.

For by raising their cries over South Tyrol today, they seem to serve national combat interests just as much as, conversely, they can most easily avoid any real struggle against the worst enemies of the German nation from within. For these patriotic, national, and partly even ethnic warriors, it is much easier, after all, to unleash their war cries against Italy in Vienna and Munich with benevolent support and in collaboration with Marxist traitors to the people and the nation than to engage in a serious fight against them themselves. Just as much has become a pretense today, so too has the entire national pretense of these people long been just an outward show, which admittedly satisfies themselves and is not perceived by a large part of our people.

Against this powerful coalition, which, from various perspectives, seeks to make the South Tyrolean question the focal point of German foreign policy, the National Socialist movement fights by steadfastly advocating for an alliance with Italy against the prevailing pro-French trend. In doing so, it emphasizes, contrary to the entire public opinion in Germany, that South Tyrol cannot and must not be an obstacle to this policy in any way. However, this view is the cause of our current foreign policy isolation and opposition and will later indeed be the cause of the resurgence of the German nation.

To justify and make this faithful belief understandable in detail, I write this work. For as little as I care to be understood by the enemies of the German people, I feel a strong obligation to strive to present and demonstrate the National Socialist fundamental ideas of a truly German foreign policy to the inherently national-minded and only poorly educated or poorly led elements of our people. I know that many of them, after honestly examining the views laid down here, will abandon their previous positions and find their way into the ranks of the National Socialist freedom movement of the German nation. They will thereby strengthen the force that will one day bring about the confrontation with those who cannot be taught because the happiness of their people is not what determines their thinking and actions, but rather the interests of their party or their own person.

———————————————— 19 ————————————————

CHAPTER 1
War & Peace

———————————————— 28 ————————————————

Politics is becoming history. History itself is the representation of the course of a people's struggle for life. I deliberately use the term 'struggle for life' here, because in truth, every struggle for daily bread, whether in peace or war, is an eternal battle against thousands and thousands of resistances, just as life itself is an eternal struggle against death. For why they live, people know as little as any other creature in the world. Only life is filled wit h the longing to preserve it. The most primitive creature [could without] knows only the self-preservation instinct of its own self, for higher beings it transfers to wife and child, for even higher ones to the entire species.

But as humans seemingly renounce their own instinct for self-preservation in favor of the species, they in truth serve it to the highest degree. For only in the renunciation of the individual often lies the guarantee of life for the community and thus again for the individual. Hence the sudden courage of the mother in defending her young and the heroic spirit of the man in the protection of his people.

The magnitude of the instinct for self-preservation corresponds to the two most powerful instincts of life: hunger and love. As the [fulfillment] quenching of eternal hunger ensures self-preservation, the satisfaction of love ensures the continuation. In truth, these two instincts are the rulers of life. And if a thousand times the fleshless aesthete protests against such an assertion, the fact of his own existence is the refutation of his protest. What is made of flesh and blood can never escape the laws that conditioned its being. As soon as the human spirit believes it is above them, it destroys that real substance which is the bearer of the spirit.

What applies to the individual human also applies to peoples. A national body is merely a multitude of more or less similar individual beings. Its strength lies in the value of the individual beings that compose it and in the nature and extent of the equality of these values. The same laws that determine the life of individuals and to which they are subject also apply to the people. Self-preservation and continuation are the great drives behind all actions, as long as such a body can still claim health. Thus, the consequences of these general laws of life for peoples among each other will be similar to those for individuals among each other.

If for every creature on this Earth the self-preservation instinct in its two goals of self-preservation and continuation represents the most elementary force, and the possibility of satisfaction is limited, then the logical consequence is the struggle in all its forms for the possibility of preserving this life, thus satisfying the self-preservation instinct.

Countless are the types of all living beings on Earth, unlimited in each individual their self-preservation instinct and the longing for continuation, whereas the space on which this entire life process takes place is limited. It is the surface of a precisely measured sphere, where the struggle of billions and billions of individual beings for life and succession occurs. This limitation of living space is the compulsion for the struggle for existence, and in this struggle lies the precondition for development.

World history in times when there were no humans was initially a representation of geological events. The struggle of natural forces with each other, the formation of a habitable surface of this planet, the separation of water and land, the shaping of mountains, plains, and seas. This is the world history of that time.

Later, with the appearance of organic life, human interest concentrates on the becoming and passing away of its myriad forms. And very late, man finally becomes visible himself, and with this, he begins to understand under the concept of world history primarily only the history of his own becoming, i.e., the representation of his own development. This development is characterized by an eternal struggle of humans against animals and against humans themselves. From the invisible chaos of individual beings, finally emerge formations, kinships, tribes, peoples, states, but the representation of their emergence and their passing away is the depiction of an eternal struggle for life.

If politics is becoming history and history itself is the representation of the struggle of humans and peoples for self-preservation and continuation, then politics is in truth the execution of a people's struggle for existence. Politics is thus not only the struggle of a people for its existence per se but for us humans the art of conducting this struggle.

As history, as the presenter of the past struggle for existence of peoples, simultaneously represents the fossilized depiction of the respective politics, it is thus also the most suitable instructor for our own political action.

If the highest task of politics is the preservation and continuation of a people's life, then [thus the life of a people is always at stake] this life is the eternal stake for which it fights, struggles, and over which decisions are made. Its task is thus the preservation [of] a substance of flesh and blood. Its success is the facilitation of this preservation. Its failure is destruction, i.e., the loss of this substance. Thus, politics is always the leader of the struggle for existence, its director, its organizer, and its effectiveness will, regardless of how humans formally designate it, [such] bring the decision over life or death of a people.

It is necessary to keep this in mind, because with it, the concepts of peace or war politics immediately dissipate into nothingness. Since the stake for which politics contends is always life, the outcome, in case of failure or success, will always be the same, regardless of the means by which politics attempts to carry out the preservation of a people's life. A peace policy that fails leads just as much to the destruction of a people, i.e., to the obliteration of its substance of flesh and blood, as a war policy that fails. In one case, the deprivation of the conditions for life causes the extinction of a people just as much as in the other. For peoples have not died out on battlefields, but lost battles have deprived them of the means for preserving existence, or better, led to their deprivation or failed to prevent it.

In general, the losses directly caused by war are in no relation to the losses of a bad and unhealthy life of a people itself. Silent hunger and poor vices kill more people in 10 years than war could in 1000 years. The cruelest war, however, is just the one that appears most peaceful to today's humanity, namely the peaceful struggle of the economy. Precisely this leads in its final consequences to sacrifices that dwarf even those of the World War. For it affects not only the living but primarily the unborn. While war in the worst case kills a fraction of the present, it murders the future. A single year of birth restriction in Europe kills more people than have fallen in all wars in Europe since the French Revolution to today, including the World War. However, this is the result of a peaceful economic policy that has overpopulated Europe without granting a number of nations the possibility of healthy development.

In general, the following should be added:

As soon as a people forgets that it is the task of politics to preserve its existence by all means and possibilities, instead wanting to subject politics to a specific mode of operation, it destroys the inner meaning of this art of guiding a people in its destiny struggle for freedom and bread.

A policy that is fundamentally warlike can keep a people away from numerous vices and diseases, but over many centuries, it will not be able to prevent a change in the inner value nonetheless. War, if it becomes a permanent phenomenon, contains an inner danger in itself, which becomes more apparent the more uneven the racial fundamental values are from which a national body is composed. This already applied in antiquity to all known states and is especially true today for all European ones.

The nature of war entails that it leads to racial selection within a people through a thousand individual processes, meaning a preferred destruction of the best elements. In countless individual cases, the call to courage and bravery is answered by the racially best and most valuable elements voluntarily signing up for special tasks or being systematically recruited through the organization of special formations. The idea of forming special legions, certain elite troops of guard regiments, and storm battalions has dominated warfare at all times.

Persian palace guards, Alexandrian elite troops, Roman Praetorian legions, lost heaps of landsknechts, guard regiments of Napoleon and Frederick the Great, storm battalions, submarine crews, and air forces of the World War all owed their existence to the same idea and the same necessity, to select from a multitude of people the correspondingly most capable men for certain peak performances and to merge them into special formations. For in the origin, every guard is not a drill troop but a combat troop. The high honor of belonging to such a community then leads to the formation of a special corps spirit, which may indeed solidify over time, eventually dissolving into superficialities.

Thus, such formations often have to bear the heaviest blood sacrifices, meaning: From a multitude of people, the most capable are selected and led to war in concentrated masses. This increases the percentage of the best dead of a people disproportionately, while conversely, the percentage of the very worst can be preserved to the highest degree. For the extreme of ideal men, ready to sacrifice their own lives for the sake of the community, stands against the number of the most miserable egoists, who see the preservation of their own purely personal life as the highest task of this life.

The hero dies, the criminal [*stays alive*] is preserved. This appears self-evident to a heroic era and especially to an idealistic youth. And it is good so, for this is proof of the still existing value of a people. The true statesman, however, must view such a fact with concern and take it into account. For what can be easily endured in one war leads to the slow bleeding of the best, most valuable part of a people in 100 wars. Thus, one may have achieved victories, but eventually, there will be no people worthy of these victories, and the wretchedness of posterity, which appears incomprehensible to many, is often the result of the successes of the past.

Therefore, a wise political leadership of a people in war must never see the purpose of a people's life as merely a means for this life. It must educate to the highest manhood, but manage the human assets entrusted to it with the utmost conscientiousness. It must not hesitate to risk the highest blood sacrifice for the existence of a people if necessary, but must always remember that peace must replace this blood someday. Wars fought for purposes that by their very nature cannot guarantee the replacement of spilled blood are violators of the national body, a sin against the future of a people.

Eternal wars can become a terrible danger for a people that possesses such unequal racial elements in its composition that only a part of it can be considered state-preserving and especially culture-creating. The culture of European peoples is based on the foundations that their Nordic blood contribution has created over the millennia. As soon as the last remnants of this Nordic blood are eliminated, the European culture will change its face, and the value of the states will decrease according to the declining value of the peoples.

A policy that is fundamentally peaceful, on the other hand, will initially allow for the preservation of the best blood carriers, but it will educate an entire people to a weakness that must fail someday as soon as the existence conditions of such a people appear threatened. They will then prefer to reduce this bread or, what is more likely, limit their own number, whether through peaceful emigration or birth control, to avoid excessive hardship in this way. Thus, a fundamentally peaceful policy becomes a scourge for a people.

For what permanent war provides on one side, emigration provides on the other. Through it, in hundreds of thousands of individual life catastrophes, a people is slowly deprived of its best blood carriers. It is sad to know that our entire national political wisdom, as far as it does not see an advantage in emigration at all, at most regrets the weakening of the number of its own people or, at best, speaks of a cultural fertilizer given to other states. What is not recognized is the heaviest [sic]. As emigration does not proceed regionally, nor is it carried out according to age groups but is left to the free play of fate, it always draws the bravest and most determined, most resistance-ready people from a people. The farmer's boy who emigrated to America 150 years ago was just as determined and daring in his village as the worker who goes to Argentina today.

The coward and weakling will prefer to die at home rather than ever muster the courage to earn his bread in unknown foreign lands. Regardless of whether need, misery, or political pressure or religious coercion weigh on people, the healthiest and most resistant will always be able to offer the most resistance. The weakling will always be the first to submit.

His preservation is usually as little gain for the victor as the left-behinds are for the motherland. Therefore, the law of action often shifts from the mother countries to the colonial lands, because a natural concentration of the highest human value has taken place there in a completely natural way. The positive gain for the new land is thus a loss for the motherland. As soon as a people has lost its best, most robust, and most natural forces through emigration over centuries, it will hardly be able to muster the inner strength to resist fate in critical times.

It will then prefer to resort to birth restriction. And here too, it is not the loss of number that is decisive, but the terrible fact that birth restriction destroys the possible highest values of a people from the outset.

For the greatness and future of a people are determined by the sum of its abilities for peak performances in all areas. These are personality values, which do not appear to be tied to the right of the firstborn. Eliminate from our German cultural life, from our science, yes, from our entire existence itself everything created by men who were not firstborns, and Germany would hardly be a Balkan state. The German people would no longer have any claim to be considered a cultural nation. It should be considered that even for those men who, as firstborns, still achieved great things for their people, it would first have to be examined whether at least one of the ancestors was not a firstborn. For if in his entire lineage even [a man the] once the firstborn appears broken, then he too belongs to those who would not exist if our ancestors had always adhered to this principle. In the life of nations, however, there are no vices of the past that are [*rights*] for the present.

The fundamentally peaceful policy, with the consequent bleeding of a national body through emigration and birth restriction, is also all the more disastrous the more it concerns a people composed of racially unequal elements. For here too, emigration will primarily deprive the people of the racially best part, while birth restriction in the homeland will also initially capture the life strata that have worked their way up due to their racial value. Gradually, their replacement will occur from the bled-out, inferior broad masses and finally, after centuries, lead to a lowering of the overall value of the people. A national body will long since no longer possess real vitality.

Thus, a policy that is fundamentally peaceful will be just as harmful and devastating as a policy that knows only war as its only weapon.

Politics must fight for the life of a people and for this life, and it must always choose the weapon of its struggle so that it serves life in the highest sense. For one does not engage in politics to be able to die, but one may only sometimes let people die so that a nation can live. The goal is the preservation of life, not the heroic death or [*even*] cowardly resignation.

---- 19 ----

CHAPTER 2
The Struggle, Not the Economy, Secures Life

---- 28 ----

The struggle for life of a people is primarily determined by the following fact:

Regardless of the cultural significance of a people, at the forefront of all life's necessities is the struggle for daily bread. Indeed, a genius leadership of a people can set great goals before them, so that they are distracted from material things, to serve outstanding spiritual ideals. In general, the interest in purely material things will increase to the extent that idealistic spiritual points of view are disappearing.

The more primitive a person is in their spiritual life, the more animalistic they become, until they finally perceive the consumption of food as the sole purpose of life. Therefore, a people can very well endure a certain limitation of material goods, as long as they are provided with a replacement in the form of sustainable ideals. However, if these ideals are not to lead to the ruin of a people, they must never take place at the expense of material nourishment, as this would threaten the health of the body politic. For a starving people will either physically collapse under the consequences of their malnutrition or must bring about a change in their situation. Physical collapse, however, sooner or later leads to mental collapse. Then all ideals cease.

Thus, ideals are healthy and correct as long as they help to strengthen the inner and general strength of a people, so that this ultimately benefits the conduct of the struggle for life. Ideals that do not serve this purpose, no matter how outwardly beautiful they may appear, are still harmful, for they move a people further and further away from the reality of life.

However, the bread a people needs to live is conditioned by the living space available to them. At least a healthy people will always try to find the satisfaction of their needs on their own soil. Any other state is sick and dangerous, even if it has made the feeding of a people possible for centuries.

World trade, global economy, tourism, etc., are all transient means of feeding a people. They depend on factors that are partly beyond the discretion and partly beyond the power of a people. The most secure foundation for the existence of a people has always been its own soil.

Now the following must be considered:

The number of a people is a variable factor. It will be increasing in a healthy people. Indeed, the increase alone can ensure the future of a people by human standards. But this also means that the demand for life's goods is growing.

The so-called internal increase in production can in most cases only suffice; to satisfy the growing demands of humanity, but not the increasing number. This is especially true for European nations. The European peoples have grown so much in their needs in recent centuries, especially in recent times, that the increase in European soil yield, which could occur from year to year in the best case, hardly keeps pace with the growth of general life necessities themselves.

The increase in number could only be compensated by an increase, thus enlargement, of living space. Now, while the number of a people is variable, the soil is a constant in itself.

This means: The increase of a people is such a natural process that it is not perceived as an extraordinary event. The increase of soil, on the other hand, is conditioned by the general distribution of ownership in the world, an act of special upheaval, extraordinary events, so that the ease of feeding a people is opposed by the extraordinary difficulty of changing space.

And yet, the regulation of the relationship between the population number and land area is of the utmost importance for the existence of a people. Indeed, one can say that the whole struggle for life of a people consists, in truth, only in securing the necessary soil for the growing population number as a general prerequisite for nourishment. For as the population continuously grows and the soil remains the same, tensions gradually arise that first manifest as a crisis, which can be compensated for a while by greater diligence, more ingenious production methods, or special frugality, but which cannot be eliminated with all these means one day. Then, the task of leading the struggle for life of a people consists in thoroughly eliminating these unbearable conditions, i.e., to bring about a tolerable relationship between population number and land area again.

There are several ways in the life of nations to correct the imbalance between population number and land area. The most natural is the adjustment of the soil from time to time to the increased population number. This requires a willingness to fight and blood sacrifice.

But this blood sacrifice is also the only one that can be justified before a people. For in gaining the necessary space for the further increase of a people from it, a multiple replacement for the humanity used on the battlefield naturally occurs. From the hardship of war then grows the bread of peace.

The sword was the pioneer of the plow, and if one wants to talk about human rights at all, then in this single case, war has served the highest right, it has given a people the land which it wants to cultivate diligently and honestly itself, so that their children may one day receive their daily bread. For this land is assigned to no one and is given to no one as a gift, but rather it is given to people as the life of providence to those who have the courage [to conquer it] in their hearts, to take possession of it, the strength to maintain it, and the diligence to plow it.

Every healthy, indigenous people therefore sees nothing sinful in acquiring land, but something natural. However, the modern pacifist, who denies this most sacred right, must first be told that he is at least feeding himself from the wrongs of past times. Further, that there is no spot on this earth that has been determined for all time as the residence of a people, since the workings of nature have forced humanity to eternal wandering over tens of thousands of years.

Finally, the current distribution of land on earth has not been carried out by a higher force, but by man himself. However, I can never regard a solution arranged by humans as an eternal value that providence now takes under its own protection and sanctifies as the law of the future. Just as the surface of the earth seems eternally subject to geological transformations, organic life allowed forms to perish in uninterrupted change to invent new ones, so is also the limitation of human dwellings subject to ongoing change.

As much as in certain times peoples may have an interest in presenting the existing world land distribution as unchangeable and binding for all the future, because it corresponds to their interests, so much will other peoples always be able to see in such a state only something universally human, which currently speaks against their favor and therefore must be changed by all means of human strength. Whoever wants to ban this struggle for all eternity from the earth, perhaps eliminates the struggle of people among themselves, but also eliminates thereby the highest driving force for their development, just as if he wanted in civil life to immortalize the wealth of certain people, the size of certain businesses forever and for this purpose would switch off the play of free forces, the competition. The result would be a disaster for a people.

The current distribution of space in the world falls in the most one-sided way so much in favor of certain peoples that they must have an understandable interest in not changing anything more about the current land distribution. But the excessive wealth of land of these peoples is contrasted with the poverty of others, who despite the most diligent effort cannot produce the daily bread necessary for life. With what higher right does one want to confront those, if they also claim a piece of land that secures their nourishment?

No. The first right in this world is the right to life, so long as one possesses the strength for it. A vigorous people will always find the ways from this right to adjust its land to its population number.

As soon as a people, whether through weakness or poor leadership, can no longer eliminate the imbalance between its grown population number and the lagging ground by increasing the land area, it will inevitably look for other ways. It will then adjust the population number to the land.

In itself, nature takes the first adjustment of the population number to the insufficient food base. Need and misery are its tools. Through them, a people can be so decimated that any further increase in number practically ceases.

The consequences of this natural adjustment of the number to the land are not always the same. Initially, a very fierce struggle for life begins among themselves, which only the strongest and most resistant individuals can endure. High child mortality on one side and high life expectancy on the other are the main signs of such a time dealing with individual lives with little regard.

As in this state everything weak is swept away by need and diseases and only the healthiest remains alive, a kind of natural selection takes place. Thus, the number of a people may be subject to a limitation, but the inner value can remain, yes, experience an inner increase. But such a process cannot last too long, otherwise the need can also turn into the opposite. The eternal food shortages can finally lead to a dull resignation to the hardship in racially not entirely homogeneous peoples, the resilience gradually decreases and instead of a selection-promoting struggle, a gradual decay occurs. This is certainly the case as soon as the human being himself, in order to steer clear of eternal hardship, no longer values an increase in his number and resorts to birth control.

Human birth control extinguishes the bearers of its highest values; emigration destroys the value of its average.

There are now two other ways in which a people can try to balance the disparity between population number and land area. The first is the increase of the internal yield of the soil, which has nothing to do with so-called internal colonization; the second is the increase of its goods production and conversion of the internal economy to an export-oriented economy.

The idea of increasing soil yield within the once set boundaries is an ancient one. The history of human soil cultivation is one of continuous progress, constant improvements, and thus increasing results. While the first part of these improvements focused on the development of soil cultivation methods and planting activity, the second part focuses on artificially increasing the soil's value by adding missing or deficient nutrients.

This line leads from the former hoe to the modern steam plow, from barnyard manure to today's synthetic fertilizers. Undoubtedly, this has infinitely increased the yield potential of the soil. But just as undoubtedly, there is a limit somewhere. Especially when considering that the standard of living of civilized humans is a general one, not determined by the amount of goods per individual of a people, but also subject to and influenced by the conditions of surrounding countries.

The modern European dreams of a standard of living derived as much from the possibilities of Europe as from the actual conditions in America. The international relations of peoples have become so easy and close through modern technology and the traffic it enables, that the European applies the conditions of American life as a standard for his own life, often without being aware of it, but forgetting that the ratio of population to land area on the American continent is infinitely more favorable than the analogous conditions of the European peoples to their living spaces. No matter how Italy or say Germany carry out the internal colonization of their soil, no matter how they increase the yield of their soil through increased scientific and methodical activity, the disparity between their number and the land, compared to the ratio of the population of the American Union to the land of the Union, remains. And if through the most diligent effort a further increase in population was possible for Germany or Italy, it would be possible to a multiple extent in the American Union. And if finally any further increase in these two European countries is definitively impossible, then the American Union can continue to grow for centuries until finally the ratio that we already have today is reached.

Especially internal colonization is based in its hoped-for effects on a fallacy. The belief that it can lead to a significant increase in soil yield is wrong. No matter how, for example, the land is distributed in Germany, whether in large or small farms or in parcels for small settlers, it changes nothing in the fact that an average of 136 people are found per square kilometer of land. This ratio is unhealthy. Feeding our people on this basis and under this assumption is not possible; it would only cause confusion if the slogan of internal colonization is presented to the masses, who then tie their hopes to it as a means to alleviate current hardship.

This would not be the case. For it is not the result of a possibly wrong type of land distribution, but the consequence of an overall insufficient amount of space currently available to our people.

Therefore, while increasing soil yield can indeed provide some relief in the life of a people for a certain time, in the long run, this will never be a relief from the obligation to readjust the insufficient living space of a people to the grown number. However, internal colonization itself can at best only lead to improvements in the sense of social reason and justice. For the overall nourishment of a people, it is of no significance.

For the foreign policy stance of a nation, however, it will often be harmful because it awakens hopes that can remove a people from realistic thinking. The ordinary honest citizen will then really believe that through diligence, industriousness, and just land distribution, he can find his daily bread at home, instead of recognizing that the strength of a people must be consolidated to gain new living space.

The economy, especially today, is seen by many as the savior from distress, worry, hunger, and misery, can indeed under certain conditions provide a people with possibilities of existence that lie outside of their relationship to their own soil and land. However, this is tied to a number of conditions that I must briefly mention here.

The purpose of such an economy is that a people produce more of certain goods of life than is necessary for their own needs, sell this surplus outside their own community, and with the proceeds, acquire those food items and also raw materials that they lack. However, this type of economy is not only a question of production but also equally a question of sales. Especially in the present, much is said about increasing production, but it is entirely forgotten that such an increase only has value as long as there is a buyer.

Within the economic life circle of a people, any increase in production will be beneficial insofar as it increases the number of goods that fall to each individual. Theoretically, every increase in industrial production of a people should lead to a reduction in the price of goods and thus to an increased consumption of the same, thereby providing individual members of the community with greater material wealth. However, in practice, this changes nothing about the fact of insufficient nutrition of a people due to inadequate soil.

For certain industrial productions can be increased, indeed multiplied, but not the production of food. As soon as a people suffers from this hardship, a remedy can only occur if a part of its industrial overproduction is able to flow outwards to replace the unavailable domestic food supplies from abroad. But then an increase in production for this purpose will only have the desired success if the buyer, specifically the foreign buyer, is found. This places the question of sales possibilities, thus the marketability, of paramount importance before us.

The sales market of today's world is not unlimited. The number of industrially active nations has continuously increased. Almost all European peoples suffer from the insufficient and unsatisfactory relationship of their soil to the population number and are therefore dependent on world exports. Recently, the American Union and in the East, Japan, have been added to this.

This automatically begins a battle for the limited market, which will become harder the more the industrially active nations increase and the more conversely the markets narrow. For while on the one hand the number of peoples competing for the world market increases, the market itself is slowly reduced, partly due to self-industrialization on their own initiative, partly through a system of branch enterprises that are being set up more and more in such countries out of pure capitalist interest.

For the following must be considered: The German people, for example, have a living interest in building ships in China on German shipyards because by doing so a certain number of people of our nationality receive the possibility of nourishment that they would not possess from our own no longer sufficient soil and land. But the German people have no interest in, say, a German financial group or even a German company establishing a so-called branch shipyard in Shanghai that now builds ships for China with Chinese workers and foreign steel, even if the company itself receives a certain profit in the form of interest or dividends. On the contrary, for the result will only be that a German financial group receives so-and-so many millions in profit, but the German national economy loses multiple times this amount due to the loss of orders.

The more pure capitalist interests begin to determine today's economy, the more general financial and stock market aspects gain decisive influence, the more this system of branch establishments will spread, thus artificially implementing the industrialization of former sales markets and especially curtailing the export opportunities of European mother countries. Today, many may still smile over this future development, but as it progresses further, in 30 years Europe will groan under its consequences.

The more the difficulties of sales grow, the more bitter will be the battle for the remaining markets. While the first weapons of this fight lie in price setting and the quality of goods, with which one tries to out-compete each other, the ultimate weapon, in the end, lies also with the sword. The so-called peaceful economic conquest of the world could only take place if the earth consisted solely of agrarian peoples and had only one industrially active economic people.

But since all major peoples today are industrial nations, the so-called peaceful economic conquest of the earth is nothing other than the battle with means that will be peaceful as long as the stronger peoples believe they can win with them, i.e., in reality, being able to kill others with peaceful economy. For that is the real result of one people's victory with peaceful economic means over another people.

One people receives through them the possibilities for life, and the other people are deprived of them. The stake here is always the substance of flesh and blood, which we call a people.

But if a truly powerful people believes it cannot defeat another with peaceful economic means, or if an economically weaker people does not want to be killed by a stronger economic power by slowly having its means of sustenance cut off, then [they will resort to force] in both cases, the fog of peaceful economic phrases will suddenly be torn apart, and war, thus the continuation of politics by other means, takes its place.

The danger of exclusive economic activity for a people lies precisely in that it too easily falls into the belief that it can definitively shape its fate through the economy, that this moves from a purely secondary position to a primary one, and finally even comes to be regarded as state-forming, robbing the people of those virtues and qualities that alone can maintain peoples and states on this earth in existence.

A particular danger of the so-called peaceful economic policy of a people lies in the fact that it initially makes an increase in population number possible, which finally bears no more relation to the life yields of its own soil and land. This overcrowding of an inadequately large living space with people often leads to severe social damages as well, as the people are now concentrated in work centers that resemble less centers of culture than abscesses on the body politic, where all evil vices, misdemeanors, and diseases seem to unite.

They are then above all breeding grounds for blood mixing and bastardization, usually resulting in racial degradation and thereby forming those purulent foci in which the international Jewish pest thrives and ensures further decomposition.

Just by this, a decline is initiated, in which the inner strength of such a people quickly fades away, all racial, moral, and ethical values fall to destruction, ideals are dismantled, and thus finally the prerequisite is removed that a people necessarily needs to be able to take the ultimate consequence in the struggle for the world market upon itself. Weakened by a vicious pacifism, the peoples will no longer be ready to fight for the sale of their goods with the investment of blood. So, as soon as a stronger party replaces peaceful economic means with the realer forces of political power, such peoples will collapse.

Then they will suffer the revenge of their own transgressions. They are overpopulated and now, due to the loss of all real prerequisites, have no more possibility to adequately nourish the excessive mass of people, no strength to break the chains of the opponents, and no inner value to bear the fate worthily. They once believed that to be able to live, thanks to their peaceful economic activity, they could renounce violence. Fate will teach them that a people is ultimately only maintained if the population number and living space stand in a certain natural and healthy ratio to each other.

That furthermore, this ratio must be reviewed from time to time, and to the extent that it shifts to the disadvantage of the land, must be restored in favor of the population number. But for this, a people needs weapons. Because acquiring land is always associated with the exertion of power.

If, however, the task of politics is the conduct of a people's struggle for life, the struggle for life of a people ultimately consists in securing the necessary amount of space for the population's nourishment, and this entire process is a question of the power exertion of a people, then the following final definition arises:

Politics is the art of conducting the struggle for life of a people for its earthly existence.

[Domestic policy] Foreign policy is the art of securing the necessary living space in size and quality for a people.

Domestic policy is the art of maintaining for a people the necessary [power content] power exertion in the form of its racial value and number.

———————— 19 ————————

CHAPTER 3
Race, Struggle, & Power

———————— 28 ————————

I want to address right here the bourgeois view that mostly sees power only as the arsenal of a nation and to a lesser extent perhaps the army as an organization. If these people's view were correct, that is, if the power of a people really lay in its possession of weapons and its army per se, then a people that has lost its army and weapons due to any circumstances would be finished forever. But these bourgeois politicians hardly believe that themselves.

Just by doubting this, they admit that weapons and military organization are things that can be replaced, hence they are not of a primary nature, but there is something above them and thus at least the source of their power. And this is indeed the case. Weapons and military forms are destructible and replaceable.

As great as their importance may be for the moment, so limited is it when viewed over longer periods. In the life of a people, the decisive factor is ultimately the will to self-preservation and the living forces available to it. Weapons can rust, forms can become outdated, but the will itself can always renew both and provide a people with whatever form the moment of need requires.

That we Germans had to deliver our weapons has a very minor significance, as far as I consider the material side of it. And that is the only side our bourgeois politicians see. The oppressive aspect of our weapons delivery lies at most in the circumstances under which it occurred, in our attitude that enabled it, and in the miserable manner of its execution that we experienced. More significant is the destruction of the organization of our army.

But even there, the main disaster is not seen in the elimination of the organization as the bearer of our weapons, but rather in the removal of an institution for educating our people to manhood, as no other state in the world possessed and indeed no people probably needed as much as our German one. The merit of our old army in the general disciplining of our people for highest achievements in all areas is immeasurable. Just our people, which in its internal racial fragmentation so much lacks the qualities that, for example, distinguish the English—cohesive standing together in times of danger—received at least a part of these qualities, which are natural and instinctively rooted in other peoples, through the path of education by the army.

The people who like to talk about socialism do not understand that the highest socialist organization at all was the German national army. Hence also the fierce hatred of the typically capitalist-oriented Judaism against an organization in which money is not identical with rank, dignity, or even honor, but performance, and in which the honor of belonging to people of a certain achievement is valued more than owning wealth and riches. A view that appears as alien as it is dangerous to the Jew, and which, if it were to become the common property of a people, would mean an immune protection against any further Jewish danger.

For example, if in the army an officer's position were to be bought, this would be understandable to Judaism. But incomprehensible, indeed eerie to it, is an organization that surrounds a man with honor who either has no fortune at all or whose income is only a fraction of another's, who is not honored or esteemed in this organization at all. And therein lay the main strength of this old incomparable institution, which, unfortunately, was also slowly beginning to be eroded in the last 30 years of peace. As it became fashionable for individual officers, especially of noble descent, to pair up with department store Jewesses, a danger arose for the old army that, if such development continued, would have turned out badly one day. In any case, there was no understanding for such occurrences in the time of Kaiser Wilhelm I. Nonetheless, all things considered, still around the turn of the century, the German army was the grandest organization in the world, and its effectiveness for our German people was more than beneficial. The breeding ground of German discipline, German efficiency, straightforward attitude, open courage, bold adventurism, stubborn persistence, and granite honesty. The concept of honor of an entire class slowly but imperceptibly became the common property of an entire people.

That this organization was destroyed by the Treaty of Versailles was all the worse for our German people as it finally gave free rein to our enemies' worst intentions internally, but our incapable bourgeoisie, lacking any genius and improvisational ability, also could not find even the most primitive replacement.

Indeed, our German people have lost possession of weapons and their bearer. But this has happened countless times in the history of nations without leading to their downfall. On the contrary: Nothing is easier to replace than a loss of weapons, and any organizational form can be recreated or renewed. What is irreplaceable is the spoiled blood of a people, the destroyed inner value.

For the current bourgeois view that the Treaty of Versailles has disarmed our people, I can only counter that the real disarmament lies in our pacifist-democratic poisoning, as well as in internationalism, which destroys and poisons the highest power sources of our people. For the source of all a people's power does not lie in its possession of weapons or in its military organization, but in its inner value, which is represented by the racial significance, that is, the racial value of a people itself, by the presence of highest individual personality values, and by its healthy attitude towards the idea of self-preservation.

When we National Socialists present this view of the true strength of a people to the public, we know that this stands against the entire public opinion today. But this is precisely the deepest meaning of our new doctrine, which separates us as a worldview from the others.

By starting from the principle that not all peoples are equal, not all people's values are equal. But if not all people's values are equal, then each people has, apart from its number as a summary value, a particular specific value that is unique to it and that cannot be completely identical to that of any other people. The effects of this particular people's value can be of the most varied types and lie in the most varied fields, but summed up they yet provide a standard for the general valuation of a people altogether. The ultimate expression of this general valuation is the historical cultural image of a people, in which the sum of all radiations of its blood value or the racial values combined in it are reflected.

This particular people's value, however, is by no means just an aesthetic-cultural one, but a general life value in itself. For it forms the life of a people in general, shapes and designs it, and thus also supplies all those forces that a people has to use to overcome life's resistances. For any cultural deed is in truth the conquest of a barbarism that has hitherto existed from the perspective of humans; every cultural creation [thus] aids in the ascent of people over their previously drawn boundaries, thereby strengthening the position of these people, so that also in the so-called cultural value of a people, in truth, lies a power for life assertion. The greater, therefore, the internal forces of a people in this direction, the stronger also the countless possibilities for life assertion in all fields of the struggle for life. The higher, therefore, the racial value of a people, the greater its general life value, [through] which it then has to use in favor of its life, in combat and in struggle with other peoples.

The significance of a people's blood value becomes fully effective only when this value is recognized, duly appreciated, and honored by a people. Peoples who do not understand this value or, due to a lack of natural instinct, no longer feel it, immediately begin to lose it. Blood mixing and racial degradation are then the consequences, which, at the beginning, are often initiated by a so-called infatuation with foreigners, in reality, an underestimation of one's own cultural values compared to those of foreign peoples.

As soon as a people no longer values the cultural expression of its own soul life determined by its blood, or even begins to feel ashamed of it, turning its senses towards foreign expressions of life, it renounces the strength that lies in the harmony of its blood and the cultural life sprouting from it. It becomes torn, uncertain in its assessment of the worldview and its expressions, loses the knowledge and feeling for its own appropriateness, to sink instead into the chaos of international conceptions, views, and the resulting cultural confusion. Then the Jew can enter in every form, and this master of international poisoning and racial corruption will not rest until he has completely uprooted and thus spoiled such a people. The end is then the loss of a specific uniform racial value and thus the final decline.

Therefore, any existing racial value of a people is ineffective, if not endangered, as long as a people does not consciously remember it and nurtures it with all care, placing all its hopes primarily on it and building upon it. Thus, the international mindset must be seen as the mortal enemy of this value. Instead, the confession to one's own people's value must fill and determine the entire life and action of a people.

As much as the true eternal factor for the greatness and significance of a people is to be sought in the people's value, so little will this value itself come into effect in its entirety if the initially dormant energies and talents of a people do not find their awakeners.

For just as humanity does not possess a uniform average value but appears to be composed of different racial values, so the value of personality within a people is not the same among all its members. Every deed of a people, whatever field it may be on, is the result of the creative action of a personality. There is no distress that finds its remedy solely through the wish of those affected by it, as long as this general wish does not find its redemption in the action of the person chosen for this task from a people. Majorities have never achieved creative accomplishments. Majorities have never provided humanity with inventions. Always, the individual person has been the founder of human progress.

Now, indeed, a people of a certain inner racial value, if this value is at all visible in its cultural or other achievements, must inherently possess the personality values, since without their appearance and creative activity, the cultural image of such a people would never have been created, and thus the possibility of any conclusion about the inner value of such a people would be missing. By mentioning the inner racial value of a people, I assess it from the sum of the achievements before me and thereby simultaneously confirm the existence of the respective personality values, which acted as representatives of the racial value of a people and created the cultural image. So much, therefore, racial value and value of personality appear intertwined because a racially worthless people can at least not receive significant creative personalities from this source, as it seems impossible conversely to conclude on an existing racial value in the absence of creative personalities and their achievements. Yet, a people can still promote or at least facilitate the effect of its personality values through the formal construction of its organism, the community of people, or the state, or even prevent it. As soon as a people appoints the majority as the ruler of its life, thus introduces democracy of today's Western conception, it will not only impair the significance of the concept of personality but also block the effectiveness of personality values. It prevents the emergence and work of individual creative persons through a formal construction of its life.

For this is the double curse of the currently prevailing democratic-parliamentary system: It is not only incapable of producing truly creative achievements itself, but it also prevents the emergence and thus the work of those men who somehow dangerously exceed the level of the average. For the majority, at all times, the most threatening person has been the one whose greatness exceeds the average measure of general stupidity, inadequacy, cowardice, but also arrogance. Moreover, through democracy, inferior individuals must become leaders almost as a matter of law, so that this system, applied consistently to any institution, devalues the entire leadership class, as far as one can still speak of such at all. This is based on the irresponsibility inherent in the nature of democracy.

Majorities are too intangible phenomena to be burdened with responsibility. The leaders appointed by them are in truth only executors of the will of the majorities. Their task is therefore less to produce genius plans or ideas and then implement them supported by an existing administrative apparatus, but rather to gather the respective majorities necessary for the implementation of certain intentions. However, the intentions tend to align with the majorities rather than the majorities with the intentions. No matter what the result of such actions may be, there is no one discernible responsible for it. This is all the more so since any real decision made is the result of numerous compromises, which will then also show in its nature and content. But who can then be held responsible?

As soon as personal responsibility is eliminated, the most compelling reason for the emergence of a powerful leadership disappears. Compare the military organization, which is highly based on the authority and responsibility of the individual, with our democratic civilian institutions, in terms of the results of both leadership training, and you will be horrified. In one case, an organization of both courageous and responsible men, proficient in their duties, in the other, cowardly incompetents. For 4 1/2 years, the German military organization withstood the greatest enemy coalition of all time. The internally democratized and decayed leadership literally collapsed at the first attempt by a few hundred scoundrels and deserters.

The poverty of the German people in truly great leading heads finds its simplest explanation in the wild disintegration we see eating away at our entire public life through the democratic-parliamentary system.

Peoples must decide. Either they want majorities or heads. Both never coexist. But greatness on this earth has always been created by heads, and what they created was then most often destroyed by majorities.

Thus, a people may well have a legitimate hope, based on its general racial value, of being able to give life to true leaders, but it must then also seek forms in the construction of its body politic that do not artificially, indeed systematically, prevent such heads from acting, erect a wall of stupidity against them, in short, do not allow them to become effective.

Otherwise, one of the most powerful sources of power for a people is buried.

[As the third factor of a people's inner strength, we have education towards self-assertion] The third factor of a people's strength is its healthy natural instinct for self-preservation. From this, numerous heroic virtues result, which alone allow a people to engage in the struggle for existence. No government will be able to achieve great successes if the people whose interests it represents are too cowardly and miserable to stand up for these interests themselves. Of course, no government should expect that a people possesses heroism if it does not educate them towards heroism itself. Just as internationalism damages and thus weakens the existing racial value, democracy destroys personality values, and pacifism paralyzes the natural forces of a people's self-preservation.

These three factors: the intrinsic value of the people, the existing personality values, and the healthy instinct for self-preservation are the sources of power from which a wise and bold domestic policy can continually draw the weapons necessary for a people's self-assertion. Then military institutions and armament technical issues will always find solutions suitable to support a people in the severe struggle for freedom and daily bread.

If the domestic political leadership of a people loses sight of these points of view or believes it only needs to arm itself technically for a conflict, then it may achieve immediate successes as much as it wants, but the future will not belong to such a people. Therefore, the task of all truly great legislators and statesmen of this world was never the limited preparation for a war, but rather the unlimited internal training and development of a people, so that according to all human reason, its future seems almost legally secured. Then wars also lose the character of individual, more or less powerful surprises, but integrate into a natural, indeed self-evident system of a thorough, well-founded, lasting development of a people.

That the current state administrations pay little attention to these viewpoints lies partly in the nature of the democracy to which they owe their existence, and on the other hand, in the fact that the state has become a purely formal mechanism, which appears to them as an end in itself, without having to cover the least with the interests of a particular people. People and state have become two different concepts. It will be the task of the National Socialist movement to bring about a fundamental change here for Germany.

---- 19 ----

CHAPTER 4
Foreign Policy Critique & Suggestions

---- 28 ----

If, therefore, the task of domestic policy—aside from the obvious satisfaction of so-called day-to-day issues—must be the hardening and strengthening of a nation's body by systematically nurturing and promoting its internal values, then the task of foreign policy must be to protect and support this internal development work of a nation's body externally and to help create and secure the general conditions for life. A healthy foreign policy must always keep in mind as its ultimate goal the acquisition of the bases of nutrition for a people. Domestic policy must secure a people the inner strength for its foreign policy assertion.

Foreign policy must secure a people's life for its domestic political development. Thus, domestic policy and foreign policy are not only closely linked but must also complement each other. The fact that in the great epochs of human history both domestic and foreign policies have adhered to other principles proves nothing for the correctness of this, but has only provided proof of the error of such actions.

Countless peoples and states have gone down as warning examples for us because they had not followed the aforementioned elementary principles. It is remarkable how little man in his life thinks about the possibility of death. How little he arranges his life individually according to the experiences that countless people before him had to make and which are all known to him.

Always, it is only exceptions who consider this and now try, due to the significance of their personality, to impose laws of life on their fellow men, which are based on the experiences of past times. It is noteworthy that countless hygienic measures, which must turn out to the benefit of a people but are inconvenient individually, have to be forcibly imposed on the public by the autocratic significance of individual persons, only to perish the moment the authority of the personality is replaced by the delusion of the masses in democracy. The average person fears death the most and in reality thinks about it the least.

The significant individual deals with it most intensively and yet fears it the least. The one lives blindly day by day, sins on, only to suddenly collapse before the all-conqueror. The other considers his coming with all care and then indeed looks into his eyes calmly and composedly.

In the life of peoples, it is the same. It is often eerie to see how little people want to learn from history, how indifferently stupid they ride over their experiences, how thoughtlessly they sin, without considering that just through their sins already so many peoples and states have perished, yes, disappeared from the earth. In general, how little they deal with the fact that even in the short span of time in which we have a historical insight, states and peoples of sometimes almost gigantic size have arisen, only to disappear without a trace 2000 years later, that world powers dominated cultural circles, of which only legend tells, giant cities have sunk into ruins, that hardly the mounds of rubble remain to show today's humanity the location of their position.

Almost beyond all imagination, however, are the worries, hardships, and sufferings of the millions and millions of individual people, who once as living substance were bearers and victims of these events. Unknown people, unknown soldiers of history. And how indifferent is the present in reality. How unfounded its eternal optimism and how destructive its deliberate ignorance, its not wanting to see and not wanting to learn.

If it were up to the broad masses, the child's play with the fire unknown to him would constantly repeat itself on the largest scale. It is therefore the task of those who feel called upon to educate a people to learn for themselves from history and now to apply their knowledge practically [now], regardless of understanding, comprehension, ignorance, or even rejection by the masses. The greatness of a man is all the more significant, the greater his courage was to lead his better insight to general victory in contrast to a commonly prevailing, but harmful opinion.

His victory will appear all the greater, the more tremendous were the resistances that had to be overcome, and the more hopeless the struggle seemed at first.

The National Socialist movement would have no right to consider itself a truly great phenomenon in the life of the German people if it did not have the courage to learn from the experiences of the past, to impose the laws of life it represents on the German people despite all resistance.

As tremendous as its internal reform work will be, it must never forget that there can be no real rise of our people in the long term if its foreign policy activity does not succeed in securing our people the general prerequisites for nutrition. It has thus become a fighter for freedom and bread in the highest sense of the word. Freedom and bread is the simplest and yet the greatest foreign policy slogan there can be for a people. The freedom to order and regulate the life of a people according to its own interests, and the bread that this people needs for its life.

If I now appear as a critic of the past and present foreign policy leadership of our people, then I am aware that the mistakes I see today were also seen by others. What might differentiate me from these is only the fact that in most cases it was just about critical realizations without practical consequences, while I strive to derive proposals for change and improvement from my insight into the errors and mistakes of the previous German domestic and foreign policy, and to form the instrument with which these changes and improvements can be realized in the future.

The foreign policy of, for example, the Wilhelminian period was felt and accordingly characterized by not a few people in Germany as disastrous in many cases. Particularly from the circles of the then Pan-German League, countless warnings came that were justified in the highest sense of the word.

I myself can empathize with the tragedy that all these warners had fallen into at the time, seeing how and what a people perishes from, and yet being unable to help.

In the last decades of the unfortunate foreign policy of the pre-war period, the parliament in Germany, that is, democracy, was not yet powerful enough to determine the heads for the political leadership of the Reich itself. This was still an imperial right, the formal existence of which no one dared to shake at that time. However, the influence of democracy had already become so strong that a certain direction seemed to be already prescribed to the imperial decisions.

This was therefore of baleful effects because now a national warner on the one hand could no longer count on being appointed to a responsible post against the declared tendency of democracy, while on the other hand, from generally patriotic ideas, he could not fight against His Majesty the Emperor with the ultimate weapon of opposition. The idea of a March on Rome would have been absurd in pre-war Germany. Thus, the national opposition was in the worst possible situation.

Democracy had not yet triumphed, but it was already in a furious fight against the monarchic state idea. The monarchic state itself did not respond to democracy's fight with the determination to destroy it, but rather with eternal concessions. Whoever took a stand against either of the two institutions ran the risk of being attacked by both.

Whoever opposed an imperial decision for national reasons was ostracized by patriotism as much as vilified by democracy. Whoever took a stand against democracy was fought by it and abandoned by patriotism. Yes, he ran the risk of being shamefully [sacrificed] betrayed by government Germany, in the sad hope that by such a sacrifice it could win Jehovah's favor and stop the Jewish press pack's mouths for a while.

As the situation was at the time, there was no prospect of getting into a responsible position in the Reich leadership against the will of democracy or against the will of His Majesty the Emperor and thus being able to change the course of foreign policy. This led to the fact that objections to German foreign policy could only be presented on paper, meaning criticism began that increasingly had to take on the characteristics of journalism. The consequence, however, was that less and less value was placed on positive proposals due to the lack of any practical feasibility, while pure critical observation gave rise to countless exhibitions, which could all the more easily be presented in full since it was hoped that this would bring down the responsible bad regime.

However, the men of criticism from back then did not achieve this. Not the regime of the time was overthrown, but the German Reich and thereby the German people fell. What they had predicted for decades had now occurred. One cannot remember these men without the deepest sympathy, who were doomed by fate to predict a collapse for 20 years and now, without having been heard and without being able to help, had to witness the most tragic catastrophe of their people.

Aged in years, embittered and bitter, yet filled with the thought that they must help, they now tried after the fall of the imperial regime to assert their influence for the resurgence of our people. This was in vain for a number of reasons.

When the revolution broke the imperial staff and raised democracy to the throne, the critics of the time were no more equipped with a weapon to overthrow democracy than they had previously been able to influence the imperial government. In their decades-long activity, they had adjusted so much to a purely literary treatment of problems that they now lacked not only the real means of power to express their opinion in a state of affairs that responded only to the outcry of the streets, but they had also lost the ability to approach the organization of a power expression that, if it was to be effective, had to be more than a written wave of protest. They all had seen the seed and the cause of the decay of the Reich in the old parties.

In the feeling of their inner integrity, they had to reject the imposition of wanting to play parties themselves far from them. Yet they could only practically implement their opinion if they were given the opportunity to have it represented by a large number. And if they wanted to shatter the parties a thousand times, they first had to form the party that sees it as its task to shatter the parties.

That this did not happen was also due to the following:

The more the political resistance of these men was forced to express itself purely journalistically, the more it adjusted to a critique that certainly exposed all the weaknesses of the then system, illuminated the faults of individual foreign policy measures, but lacking any possibility of personal responsibility, omitted positive proposals all the more as naturally in political life there is no action that does not have its downsides as well as its bright sides.

There is no foreign policy combination that can ever be considered completely satisfactory. The critic, whose main task, as things were at the time, had to be seen in the removal of the regime recognized as incapable as a whole, had no reason to come up with positive proposals besides the useful critical examination of the actions of this regime, which due to their associated concerns could have been subjected to critical scrutiny just as easily. The critic will never want to weaken the significance of his criticism by making proposals that could themselves be subjected to criticism.

Gradually, however, the purely critical thinking passed so deeply into the flesh and blood of the then representatives of the national opposition that even today they view and deal with both domestic and foreign policy critically, only critically. They have remained critics for the most part, which is why even today they cannot come to a clear, unambiguous positive decision either domestically or foreign policy-wise, partly due to their own uncertainty and indecisiveness, but also partly due to the fear of thus providing cheap material for their opponents' criticism. Thus, they want improvements in a thousand things but cannot decide on a single step because even this step again does not satisfy completely, has concerning aspects, in short, has its downsides, which they recognize and which frighten them.

Now, healing a people's body from deep and severe illnesses is not about finding a prescription that is completely free of poison, but often about breaking one poison with an antidote. One must have the courage to implement and execute decisions to remove conditions recognized as deadly, even if they themselves carry dangers. As a critic, I have the right to examine all foreign policy options and individually pick apart each according to the concerning aspects or possibilities they carry. As a political leader who wants to make history, I must decide on a path, even if a thousand times sober consideration tells me that it carries certain dangers and that it may not lead to a possibly completely satisfying end.

I cannot forgo success just because it is not one hundred percent certain. I must not refrain from a step because it may not be complete if the place I currently stand on will definitely bring my absolute demise soon. I must also not reject a political action just because it will bring benefits to my people as well as another people. Indeed, I must not even do this if the benefit for the other will be greater than for my own, if in the case of non-action the disaster of my people is absolutely certain.

Today, precisely due to the purely critical viewpoint of many people, I am presented with the most severe resistances. They acknowledge this and that as good and correct, but still, they cannot participate because this and that are concerning. They know that Germany and our people will perish, but they cannot join the rescue action because they also find this or that in it, which at least is a flaw. In short, they see the decline and lack the resolve to oppose it because some concerning possibility is already discerned in the resistance and in the action itself.

This sad mentality gives rise to another evil. Today, there are not a few, especially so-called educated people, who, if they decide to support or even promote a certain action, first carefully weigh how many percent chances of success there are, and then calculate the size of their commitment also according to these percentages. That means: because, for example, some foreign or domestic political decision is not completely satisfying and does not seem entirely sure to succeed, one must not fully represent it with full commitment of all energy. These unfortunate individuals have no understanding that, on the contrary, a decision that I deem necessary in itself but whose success is not completely certain, or whose success will only offer partial satisfaction, must be fought through with increased energy, that what is lacking in percentage chances of success must be compensated by energy in execution.

Thus, the only question to be examined is whether a situation requires a particular decision or not. Once such a decision has been definitively determined and recognized as necessary, its implementation must proceed with the utmost ruthlessness and highest energy expenditure, even if a thousand times the final result itself will again be unsatisfactory or in need of improvement or might occur with only a low percentage probability.

If a person appears to be afflicted with cancer and must die without a doubt, it would be absurd to refuse an operation because it either only succeeds with a low percentage of certainty, and the patient, even in case of success, will still not be a 100 percent healthy person. Much more absurd, however, would it be if the doctor himself carried out the operation with limited or half-hearted energy due to these limited prospects. Yet, these people continuously expect this most absurd in internal and foreign political matters. Because a political operation is not entirely certain in success or will not be entirely satisfactory in result, they not only forego its implementation but also expect, in case it takes place anyway, that it at least occurs with restrained forces, without complete commitment, always in the quiet hope of perhaps being able to keep a back door of retreat open. This is the soldier who is attacked in the open field by a tank and [because of] considering the uncertainty of the success of his resistance, conducts it from the outset with only half strength. His backdoor is flight, and his end is certain death.

No, the German people today are attacked by a pack of predatory enemies both inside and outside. The continuation of this situation is our death. Every possibility to break it must be seized, and if its result a thousand times will also have weaknesses or concerning sides. [Whoever is fallen to the devil has little choice in his allies] And each such possibility must be fought through with utmost energy.

The success of the Battle of Leuthen was uncertain, but the fight was necessary. Frederick the Great did not win because he faced his enemies with only half his strength, but only because he compensated for the uncertainty of success with the excess of his genius, the boldness and decisiveness of his commands, and the daring with which his regiments fought.

I indeed fear that I will never be understood by my bourgeois critics, at least not until success proves the correctness of our actions. The common man has a better [instinct] advisor here. He replaces the cunning wisdom of our intellectuals with the certainty of his [feeling] instinct and the faith of his heart.

However, when I deal with foreign policy in this work, I do so not as a critic but as the leader of the National Socialist movement, which I know will make history one day. If I am still forced to critically examine the past and the present, it is only to justify and make understandable our own positive path. Just as the National Socialist movement practices criticism domestically but possesses its own ideologically founded program, so it also has to recognize not only what others have done wrong in foreign policy but to derive its own actions from this recognition.

Thus, I know exactly that even our highest success will not create 100 percent happiness because, given the inadequacy of people and the resulting general circumstances, the ultimate perfection always lies only in the programmatic theory. I also know further that no success is achieved without sacrifice, just as no victory is won without personal losses.

However, the recognition of the imperfection of a success will never prevent me from preferring such an imperfect success to the recognized perfect downfall. I will then commit myself, try to compensate for what is lacking in the probability of success or the magnitude of success with greater determination, and transfer this spirit to the movement I lead. Today we fight against a hostile front that we must and will break through.

We assess our own sacrifices, weigh the magnitude of the possible success, and will proceed to attack, regardless of whether it will come to a halt 10 or 1000 kilometers behind the current lines. Because wherever our success ends, it will always only be the starting point for a new fight.

---------- 19 ----------

CHAPTER 5
The Policy of the NSDAP

---------- 28 ----------

I am a German nationalist. This means, I profess allegiance to my ethnic group. My entire thinking and acting belongs to it.

I am a socialist. I see before me not class or status, but those communities of people who are connected by blood, united by a language, subject to a common fate. I love the people and only hate its respective majorities, because I see in them neither a representative of the greatness nor the happiness of my people.

The National Socialist movement that I lead today aims at the liberation of our people both internally and externally. It intends to give our people internally those forms of life that seem adapted to its nature and to benefit it as an expression of this nature. Thus, it aims to preserve the nature of this people and to breed higher through systematic promotion of its best people and virtues.

It stands for the external freedom of this people because only under it can this life find a shape that is beneficial to the people themselves. It fights for the daily bread of this people because it defends this people's right to life [in hunger]. It fights for the necessary space because it represents the life rights of this people.

Therefore, the National Socialist movement understands by the term domestic policy the promotion, strengthening, and consolidation of our people's existence through the introduction of life forms and life laws that correspond to the essence of our people and are able to bring its fundamental forces into effect.

It understands by foreign policy the security of this development through the preservation of freedom and procurement of the most necessary prerequisites for life. Thus, in terms of foreign policy, the National Socialist movement differs from the previous bourgeois parties as follows: The foreign policy of the national bourgeois world has always been merely a border policy, whereas the foreign policy of the National Socialist movement will always be a space policy. The German bourgeoisie, in its boldest plans, may reach the unification of the German nation, but in reality, it mostly gets lost in amateurish border adjustments.

The National Socialist movement, on the other hand, will always determine its foreign policy by the necessity to secure the necessary space for the life of our people. It knows no Germanizing or Germanification, as is the case with the national bourgeoisie, but only an expansion of its own people. It will never see a national or even racial strengthening in the subjugated so-called Germanized Czech or Pole, but a racial weakening of our people. Because its concept of nationality is not determined by previous patriotic state ideas, but rather by racial, folkish insights.

Thus, the starting point of its thinking is entirely different from that of the bourgeois world. Many things that appear to the national bourgeoisie as political successes of the past and present are for us either a failure or the cause of later misfortune. And much that we consider self-evident appears to the German bourgeoisie as incomprehensible or even horrific.

Yet, I know that particularly a part of the German youth from bourgeois circles will be able to understand me. And neither I nor the National Socialist movement count on finding support from the circles of today's active political-national bourgeoisie, but we do know that at least a part of the youth will find their way into our ranks.

For them

— 19 —

CHAPTER 6
From National Unification
To Spatial Policy

— 28 —

The question of a people's foreign policy is determined by factors that partly lie within a people and are partly given by the environment. The internal factors are generally reasons for the necessity of a particular foreign policy and the extent of the power available for its implementation. Peoples on impossible terrain will fundamentally, at least as long as they are healthily led, always strive to expand their territory, thus their living space.

This process, originally based solely on the concern for food, appeared so beneficial in its successful resolution that it gradually gained the glory of success in itself. That is, space expansion, which had its first reason in pure practicalities, became over the course of human development a heroic act that then took place even when the original prerequisites or causes were lacking. The attempt to adapt the living space to the increased population number later became unmotivated wars of conquest, which carried the seed of a later backlash due to their lack of motivation.

The response to this is pacifism. There has been pacifism in the world ever since there have been wars that no longer had their meaning in the conquest of land for the feeding of a people. Since then, it has become the eternal companion of war. It will disappear again as soon as war has ceased to be an instrument for the booty or power hunger of individuals or peoples, and as soon as it becomes again the last weapon with which the people fight for their daily bread.

However, the expansion of a people's living space for breadwinning will also require the entire effort of a people in the future. If it is the task of domestic policy to prepare this effort, then it is the task of foreign policy to conduct it in such a way that the highest possible success seems assured. This is conditioned not only by the strength of the people wanting to act but also by the power of the resistances. The disproportion of the power of the peoples struggling with each other for land always leads to the attempt to appear either conquering themselves through alliances or to resist the overpowering conqueror.

This marks the beginning of alliance politics.

After the victorious war of 1870/71, the German people had achieved an infinitely respected position in Europe. A large number of German states, which had previously been only loosely connected and often stood hostile to each other in history, were united into one empire, thanks to the successes of Bismarck's statecraft and Prussian-German military performance. A province of the old German empire, lost 170 years earlier and finally annexed by France in a shortened robbery procedure, returned to the motherland. Numerically, this united the majority of the German nation, at least in Europe, into a single state entity. It was worrying that this state entity enclosed millions of Poles and . . . . . Frenchified Alsatians and Lorrainers. This neither corresponded to the idea of a national state nor that of a racial state. The national state, from a bourgeois perspective, had to ensure at least the uniformity of the state language, down to the last school and the last street sign. It further had to integrate these people into German thought in education and life, and make them bearers of this thought.

This was attempted weakly, perhaps never seriously wanted, and the opposite was achieved in practice.

Conversely, a racial state must under no circumstances annex Poles with the intention of wanting to make Germans out of them one day. On the contrary, it had to decide either to isolate these racially foreign elements to avoid continually dissolving the blood of its own people, or it had to simply remove them and transfer the thus vacated land to its own people.

That a bourgeois-national state was incapable of such action is, of course, self-evident. There was never any thought given to it, nor would such a thing have ever been done. But even if the will had been present, the power would not have been sufficient to carry it out, less because of the reactions from the rest of the world and more due to the complete lack of understanding such an action would have found among the ranks of the so-called national bourgeoisie. The bourgeois world once believed it could overthrow the feudal system, while in reality, it only continued its mistakes through bourgeois moneybags, [professors] lawyers, and journalists. It has never possessed an idea of its own, but an immense amount of pretension and money.

With that alone, one can neither overcome nor build a world. Hence, the period of bourgeois governance in world history will be as short as it is shamefully pitiful.

Initially, the establishment of the empire also incorporated toxins into the new state body, whose destructive effect was all the more inevitable as, to make matters worse, bourgeois equality gave Jews the opportunity to use it as their safest shock troops.

Apart from that, the empire, although it covered the largest part, only captured a section of the German nation. It would have been natural that if the new state had no great foreign policy goal of a racial nature, then at least as a so-called bourgeois national state, its smallest foreign policy goal should have been the further unification and consolidation of the German nation.

Something the bourgeois, national, Italian state never forgot.

Thus, the German people received a national state that did not fully encompass the nation in reality.

Hence, the new empire borders were incomplete from a national policy perspective. They cut across the German language area, through parts that had at least formerly belonged to the German Confederation, albeit in the loosest form.

Even more unsatisfactory were these new borders from a military standpoint. Everywhere unprotected, open areas, which, especially in the West, were of decisive importance for German economics far beyond the border regions. These borders were militarily disadvantageous as [on the margin] several major states with equally aggressive foreign policy goals and extensive military resources surrounded Germany. Russia in the East, France in the West. Two military states, one eyeing East and West Prussia, while the other tirelessly pursued its centuries-old foreign policy goal of establishing a Rhine border. Then there was England, the most powerful maritime force on Earth. As vast and unprotected as the German land borders were in the East and West, so unfavorably constrained was the possible operational base for naval warfare. Nothing facilitated the combat against the German submarine warfare more than the spatially conditioned constriction of its operating area. The wet triangle was easier to block and monitor than it would have been for a coast of, say, 600 or 800 km in length. All in all, the new empire borders, from a military standpoint, had nothing satisfactory about them. Nowhere a natural obstacle or natural protection. But everywhere militarily advanced power states with foreign political intentions hostile to Germany. Bismarck's premonition that the new empire he founded would have to defend its existence with the sword once more was deeply founded.

Bismarck stated what came to fruition 45 years later.

Thus, the new imperial borders could not be sufficient from national and military-political perspectives. Yet, they were even more insufficient from the standpoint of the nutritional possibilities for the German people. Germany has always been an overpopulated area. This was due to the nature of the German people's encirclement in Central Europe on one hand, and the cultural and factual significance of this people and its human fertility on the other. The German people have always been in a space crisis since their historic entrance into world history. Indeed, their very first political appearance was forced by this need. And since the beginning of the migration period, our people have never been able to eliminate their space shortage except through sword conquest or through their own population reduction. This population reduction was soon handled by hunger, emigration, many times endless unfortunate wars, and in recent times by voluntary birth control.

The wars of 1864, 1866, and 1870/71 had their purpose in the national-political unification of a part of the German people and thereby definitively ending the German fragmentation in state politics. Hence, the flag of the new empire, black-white-red, had no ideological significance whatsoever but was purely German-national in the sense of overcoming the previous state-political rift. The black-white-red flag thus became the symbol of the German federal state that overcame division. The fact that it, nevertheless and despite its youth, enjoyed almost divine reverence was due to the nature of its inauguration, which also significantly elevated the birth of the empire itself above similar events otherwise. Three victorious wars, the last of which became a veritable wonder of German statecraft, German military leadership, and German heroism, are the deeds from which the new empire arose. And when it finally announces itself to the world through its greatest imperial herald in the Imperial Proclamation, [roaring] the sound of the Paris siege front's batteries rings in the music of the fanfares.

Never before was an empire proclaimed in such a manner.

However, the black-white-red flag appeared to the German people as the symbol of this unique event, just as the black-red-yellow will remain the symbol of the November Revolution.

As much as under this flag the German states gradually merged and the new empire ensured them state-political significance and recognition externally, the foundation changed little about the main plight, the lack of space for our people. The greatest military-political deeds of our people did not manage to give the German people a border within which it could sustain itself. On the contrary: As the new empire enhanced the prestige of Germanhood, it became harder for individuals to turn their backs on such a state as emigrants, while conversely, a certain national pride and a now almost incomprehensible joy of life led to seeing joy in having many children not as a burden but rather as something delightful.

Since the year 1870/71, the population increase in Germany was visibly rapid. In part, its nourishment was covered by the diligent hard work and great scientific proficiency with which the German now cultivated his fields within the secured boundaries of his nation. However, a large part, if not the greatest, of the increase in German soil production was consumed by an equally significant increase in the general standards of living that the citizen of the new state now also demanded. The people of sauerkraut eaters and potato consumers, as the French scornfully called them, began to slowly adapt their standard of living to that of the rest of the world. Thus, only a portion of the results of the increase in German agriculture remained available for the pure population increase.

In fact, the new empire never knew how to banish need. Even in the new empire, the attempt was initially made to maintain the ratio between population and land area within possible limits through continuous emigration. Because the most striking proof of the correctness of our assertion for the overriding importance of the relationship between population number and land area lies in the fact that due to this disproportion, especially in Germany during the 70s, 80s, and 90s, the need led to an emigration epidemic that swelled to figures of nearly 1.25 million people per year at the beginning of the 90s.

Thus, the food problem of the German people was not solved even for the existing mass of people by the new imperial foundation. However, any further increase in the German nation could not occur without such a solution. Regardless of how this solution turned out, it had to be found in any case, and the most important problem of German foreign policy after the year 1870/71 had to be the question of solving the food problem.

───────────────── 19 ─────────────────

CHAPTER 7
The Failed Economic & Alliance Policy of the Second Empire

───────────────── 28 ─────────────────

Under the countless proclamations of Bismarck, there is hardly one that the bourgeois political world would have preferred to quote more than the one saying that politics is the art of the possible. This phrase had a greater appeal, the smaller were the political spirits that had to manage the legacy of the great man. Because with this sentence, even the most pitiful political bunglers could be adorned, or even justified, by simply referring to the great man himself and attempting to prove that something other than what was being done was not possible at the moment, and that politics, however, is the art of the possible, thus acting in Bismarck's spirit and in Bismarck's sense. With this, even a Mr. Stresemann could achieve something of an Olympian stature, if not Bismarckian, at least also bald-headed.

Bismarck had a precisely delineated and clearly defined political goal. It is outrageous to claim that he achieved his life's work only through an accumulation of various political possibilities and not through mastering the respective situations with an overarching political goal in mind. Bismarck's political goal was the resolution of the German question through blood and iron, elimination of the Austro-Prussian dualism, establishment of a new German empire under Prussian-Hohenzollern leadership, maximum possible security of this empire from external threats, and organization of its internal administration following the Prussian model. In following this goal, Bismarck utilized every opportunity, worked with the tools of diplomatic art as long as they promised success, and threw the sword into the scales when only force could bring about a decision. A master of politics, whose operational area for Bismarck ranged from the salon parquet to the blood-soaked earth of the battlefield.

This was the master of the politics of possibilities.

His successors had neither a political goal nor even a political thought; they floundered from today to tomorrow and from tomorrow to the day after, then with unfounded audacity referred themselves to that man, whom they themselves, or their intellectual predecessors, had caused the severest worries and bitterest struggles, to represent their politically meaningless and disastrous babbling as the art of the possible.

As Bismarck, with his three wars and all thanks to his genius political activity, had established the new empire, this was the highest achievement that could initially be achieved at all. It was also the absolutely necessary prerequisite for any future political representation of our people's life interests. Without the creation of the new empire, the German people would never have experienced the power shaping that would have been essential for conducting the fight of destiny also in the future.

It was equally clear that the new empire, initially forged on the battlefield, needed time to become accustomed to each other internally. Years of adaptation had to pass until this unification of German states into a confederation could become a real federal state. This was the time when the iron chancellor shed the cuirassier boots to now, with infinite wisdom, patience, wise understanding, and wonderful feeling, replace the pressure of Prussian hegemony with the power of trust. The achievement of turning a states' coalition formed on the battlefield into a Reich united by touching love is among the greatest ever accomplished by political art.

That Bismarck initially limited himself to this was as much in the wisdom of his insight as it was a fortune for the German nation. These years of peaceful internal expansion of the new empire were necessary unless one wanted to succumb to a conquest mania whose results would have been all the more uncertain as the executive force internally would have lacked the homogeneity necessary for assimilating further territories.

Bismarck reached his life goal. He solved the German question, eliminated the Austro-Prussian dualism, raised Prussia to the leading German power, united the nation thereafter, consolidated the new empire internally within the limits of what was then possible, and shaped its military protection in such a way that this whole process of internal German empire re-founding, which now had to last for decades, could not be significantly disturbed by anyone.

As Bismarck, the elder ex-Chancellor, could look back on the completed work of his life, this work by no means represented the conclusion of the life of the German nation. Through Bismarck's re-establishment of the empire, the German nation had found, after centuries of state decay, an organic form that not only united the German people but also gave these united individuals a form of power expression that was both real and idealistic in nature. If the flesh and blood of this people were the substance whose preservation must be attempted in this world, then the new Reich had become the instrument of power through which the nation could henceforth assert its right to live among the rest of the world.

It was the task of the post-Bismarck era to decide on the further steps that needed to be taken in the interest of preserving the German people's substance.

These decisions, which had to be fundamental in nature and thus signified a new goal setting, would then dictate the further specific political work. That is to say, just as Bismarck as an individual had set a goal for his political actions, which then allowed him to proceed from case to case using all available means to achieve these goals, so too the post-Bismarck era needed to set a specific goal that was both necessary and possible to achieve, which the interests of the German people imperatively required. And to achieve this goal, one could indeed utilize all possible means, ranging from the arts of diplomacy to the art of war.

However, this goal-setting did not occur.

It's not necessary to list all the reasons, and probably impossible to identify all the factors that caused the omission of further strategic planning after the new Reich was established by Bismarck. A major reason was undoubtedly the absence of a political figure of genius. But almost as significant were issues intrinsic to the nature of the new Reich itself.

Germany had become a democratic state, and although the Reich's leadership was in the hands of the Kaiser, these decisions could hardly escape the influence of the general opinion reflected in parliamentary institutions, shaped by political parties and a press influenced by unseen puppeteers. Thus, the interests of the nation receded behind the interests of specific groups. This was exacerbated by the lack of clear understanding among the general public about the nation's real interests, in contrast to the concrete interests of specific political parties or the media world.

Although now a national state, the concept of national sentiment remained merely state-patriotic-dynastic, barely touching upon ethnic or racial insights. Hence, there was general confusion about the future direction of foreign policy. From a national standpoint, the state's next task after its internal construction should have been the continuation and completion of national unification. No goal should have been more obvious than the annexation of German-speaking areas in Europe, which were historically integral not just to the German nation but to a German empire.

However, such a straightforward goal was not pursued, partly due to other resistances but also because the concept of 'nation' was too vague, too little considered to sufficiently motivate such a step. It would have conflicted with patriotic-legitimist notions and sympathies. An authentic national state would have considered the incorporation of Germany's old Eastern Marches a logical next step, but this was hindered not just by a lack of national understanding but also by the specific interests of certain groups.

Centrist circles, for instance, wanted at all costs a policy that maintained the so-called Catholic Habsburg state, hypocritically speaking of 'tribal brothers' while knowing that these very brothers were being suppressed within the Habsburg monarchy. For the Centre, even in Germany, it wasn't German perspectives that mattered. Every Pole, every Alsatian traitor, and Francophile was preferable to a German who wouldn't join such a treacherous organization.

Thus, in shaping Germany's ill-advised foreign policy, the Centre — professing to represent Catholic interests — contributed to undermining the principal stronghold of a truly Christian worldview, Germany. Under the pretext of defending Catholic interests, this party has helped during peace times to weaken and destroy the main bastion of a real Christian worldview, Germany. They partnered with declared god-deniers, atheists, and blasphemers whenever it served to damage the German national state and thus the German people.

Similarly, the Social Democracy, representing Marxist ideology at the time, resisted anti-Habsburg politics, though for different reasons. But the ultimate goal was the same for both parties: to damage Germany as much as possible. Both the Centre and Marxist Social Democracy operated under a mindset that the weaker the state, the more unchecked and profitable their leadership would become.

If the old Reich wanted to resume the consolidation of German people in Europe for national-political reasons, it would necessarily have to consider the dissolution of the Habsburg conglomerate of states, which would naturally lead to forming a new grouping of European powers with similar interests. This could have led to a European coalition that might have determined the fate of Europe for decades. However, this would have required the actual dissolution of the Triple Alliance (Dreibund), which, although practically already defunct, remained officially intact.

The alliance with Austria-Hungary made sense for Germany as long as it could hope for an increase in power in times of danger through this alliance. It became senseless the moment the military gain was less than the military burden it imposed on Germany. From the very first day of the Triple Alliance, this was the case if, as a result of the alliance, Russia became Germany's adversary. Bismarck weighed this carefully and therefore arranged the so-called Reinsurance Treaty with Russia, which essentially meant that if Germany were driven into a conflict with Russia due to its alliance with Austria, it would let Austria go. This showed that Bismarck recognized the problematic nature of the Triple Alliance and made necessary provisions for all eventualities with his policy of possibilities.

The Reinsurance Treaty once contributed to the dismissal of the greatest German statesman of modern times. However, since the occupation of Bosnia by Austria-Hungary and the resulting surge in Pan-Slavic movement, the situation Bismarck feared occurred in the early 1890s. The alliance with Austria brought enmity with Russia, a situation which was the root cause why Marxism, while not necessarily supporting German foreign policy, made any other direction virtually impossible.

The relationship between Austria and Italy was always essentially the same. Italy initially joined the Triple Alliance out of caution against France, not out of love for Austria. On the contrary, Bismarck accurately recognized the internal warmth of the Italian-Austrian relationship when he stated that there were only two possible states between Austria and Italy: either alliance or war.

Real sympathy in Italy—aside from a few Francophile fanatics—existed only for Germany. And that was understandable. It reflects the utter political ignorance and naivety of the German people, especially its so-called bourgeois-national intelligentsia, that they believed it possible to transfer the legalistic Triple Alliance into the realm of friendly affection.

This was not even the case between Germany and Austria, for even here the Triple Alliance, or more correctly the alliance with Germany, was genuinely embraced only in the hearts of a relatively small portion of the Germans in Austria. The Habsburgs would never have joined this Triple Alliance if there had been another way to preserve their decaying state. When, in the July days of 1870, the German people flared up in outrage under the outrageous provocation of France and rushed to protect the German Rhine, hoping for the moment of revenge for Sadowa in Vienna, one meeting followed another, one crown council succeeded the next, couriers flew back and forth, and the first call-up orders were issued.

However, the first news from the front had already arrived, and only after Weißenburg came Wörth, after Wörth came Gravelotte, Metz, Mars la Tour, and finally Sedan, did the Habsburgs, under the pressure of the newly liberated German opinion shouting out in relief, begin to discover their German hearts as well. Had Germany lost the first battles at that time, then the Habsburgs, along with Austria, would have done what they later reproached Italy for.

And what they indeed intended to do for the second time during the World War and committed as the basest betrayal against the state that had drawn its sword for them. For and because of this state, Germany endured the gravest bloodshed, and from this state, it was betrayed not just in a thousand individual cases but finally by the representative himself, all things and truths that our bourgeois national patriotism prefers to conceal, to be able now to shout against Italy.

If the House of Habsburg later crept into the Triple Alliance, it was really only because without the Triple Alliance, this house would have long been swept away to where it finds itself today. However, when I contemplate the sins of this house in the history of the German people, one thing painfully appears to me: God's mill this time was driven by forces outside the German people.

Moreover, the Habsburgs had every reason to seek an alliance, especially with Germany, because this alliance, in reality, meant the abandonment of German identity in Austria. The Habsburgs' policies of denationalization in Austria, their Czechification and Slavicization of German identity, would never have been possible had not the Empire itself held its moral umbrella over them. For what right did the German-Austrian have to protest against a state policy, for national reasons, that was supported by the epitome of the German national idea as it was embodied for the German-Austrian in the Empire?

And conversely, could Germany exert any pressure to prevent the gradual de-Germanization in Austria if the Habsburgs themselves were allies of the Empire? One must know the weakness of the political leadership of the Empire to understand that anything else would have been more likely than even the attempt of a truly vigorous influence on the ally that would have affected its internal conditions. The cunning Habsburgs knew this very well, as the Austrian diplomacy was far superior to the German in cunning and slyness. Conversely, this German diplomacy, as if struck with blindness, seemed to have no idea of the events and conditions within its ally. Only the war then probably opened the eyes of most.

However, this very friendliness of the Habsburgs towards the alliance was all the more disastrous for Germany, as it ensured the final undermining of the conditions for this alliance. Because now the Habsburgs, calmly and without fear of German interference, were able to extinguish German identity in Austria, the value of this entire alliance for Germany itself became increasingly problematic. What was an alliance supposed to mean for Germany, one that was never seriously intended by the ruling house, since the House of Habsburg would never have considered the case of an alliance to also regard German interests as given, and under whose effectiveness the only real friends of this alliance had to slowly succumb to de-Germanization. For in the rest of Austria, the alliance was at best seen as indifferent, but in most cases, it was internally despised.

Even the press in Vienna, the capital, was much more pro-French than pro-German oriented in the last 20 years before the war. The press of the Slavic provinces, however, was consciously hostile to Germany. In the same measure, however, as the Habsburgs culturally promoted Slavic identity whenever possible, and now these provinces received centers of their own national culture, centers of a particular political will also emerged. It is the historical punishment for the House of Habsburg not to have seen that this ethnic animosity, initially mobilized against the German people, would one day consume the Austrian state itself.

The alliance with Austria had become particularly nonsensical for Germany at the moment when, thanks to the work of the treacherous German-Austrian Marxism, the so-called universal suffrage had definitively broken the dominance of German identity in the Austrian state. Because, in reality, German identity constituted only one-third of the population of Cisleithania, the Austrian half of the Austro-Hungarian state. As soon as universal suffrage became the basis of the Austrian representation, the situation of German identity became hopeless, especially since the clerical parties did not want to consciously represent national viewpoints any more than they were consciously betrayed by the Marxists.

The same Social Democracy that hypocritically speaks of German identity in South Tyrol today shamelessly betrayed and sold out German identity in old Austria at every opportunity. They always stood on the side of the enemies of our people. The most brazen Czech presumption has always found its representatives in the so-called German Social Democracy. Every act of German oppression received their approval. And every instance of German retreat saw the German Social Democracy as a collaborator. What could Germany expect from a state whose political leadership, particularly as expressed in parliament, was consciously and deliberately anti-German to the extent of 4/5?

The benefits of the alliance with Austria truly lay only on Austria's side, while Germany had to bear the disadvantages. And they were not few.

The nature of the Austrian state meant that a number of neighboring states had as their goal the dissolution of Austria in their national policies. For what the post-Bismarckian era in Germany never accomplished, even the smallest Balkan states possessed: namely, a specific foreign policy goal that they sought to achieve with and after all means available to them. All these newly emerged national states bordering Austria saw their highest political future task in liberating the ethnic compatriots who lived under Austria's and Habsburg's rule.

It was obvious that this liberation could only come through military confrontations, and that it would lead to the dissolution of Austria as well. An obstacle to this was the Austrian resistance itself, which was even less effective as it relied primarily on those it sought to liberate. In the event of a coalition war involving Russia, Romania, and Serbia against Austria, the northern and southern Slavic elements were automatically excluded from Austrian resistance, leaving only Germans and Hungarians as the main combatants.

However, experience has shown that the withdrawal of certain combat forces for ethnic reasons leads to a breakdown and thus paralysis of its front altogether. On its own, Austria would have had very little resistance to offer in such a general offensive war. This was well understood both in Russia and in Serbia, in Romania as well. What kept Austria going was only the powerful ally it could rely on. But what could be more natural than the belief forming in the minds of the Austrian-hostile leading statesmen as well as in public opinion that the way to Vienna must therefore lead through Berlin?

The more states thought to succeed Austria and couldn't due to German solidarity, the more enemies Germany itself had to contend with. Around the turn of the century, the weight of these opponents brought about by Austria against Germany was many times greater than the possible military assistance Austria could ever provide for Germany.

Thus, the inner sense of this alliance policy was completely reversed. The situation was further complicated by the third ally, Italy. As mentioned earlier, Italy's relationship with Austria was never a matter of the heart, hardly even one of reason, but rather simply the result and consequence of overpowering pressure. Above all, the Italian people and intellectuals were always capable of harboring sympathies for Germany.

An alliance between Italy and Germany alone had all the reasons in its favor around the turn of the century. The notion that Italy would inherently be disloyal as an ally is so stupid and foolish that only the politicos of our apolitical so-called national bourgeoisie can come up with it. The most striking counterproof is provided by the history of our own people, namely, when Italy was once allied with Germany, albeit against Austria. Of course, the Germany of that time was led by the genius of Bismarck's Prussia and not the Reich maltreated by the political incompetence of later bunglers.

Certainly, Italy suffered defeats on the battlefields on land and at sea, but it honorably fulfilled its duties as an ally, unlike Austria in the World War into which Germany was dragged by Austria. For when Italy was offered a separate peace that would have given it everything it could later achieve, it proudly and indignantly rejected it, despite the military defeats it suffered, while the Austrian leadership not only hungered for such a separate peace but was ready to let all of Germany go. If it did not come about, it was not due to the character strength of the Austrian state but rather the nature of the demands that the adversary placed on it, demands that in practice meant its dissolution.

However, the fact that Italy in 1866 suffered military defeats could not really be interpreted as a sign of disloyalty to the alliance. Surely, victories would have been preferable to defeats, but Italy at that time could not be compared to the Germany of that time or later, because it lacked that overwhelming military crystallization power that Germany had in Prussia. A German alliance without the foundation of the Prussian military power would have been just as inferior to the attack of such an old and at that time not yet nationally decayed military power as Austria possessed, as was the case with Italy. However, the essential point was that the Italy of that time facilitated the decision in Bohemia in favor of the future German Empire by tying up a significant and large part of the Austrian army. For anyone who considers the critical situation on the day of the Battle of Königgrätz, it cannot be claimed that it would have been indifferent to Germany's fate whether Austria had been on the battlefield with 140,000 more men, as it could be due to the Italian engagement.

Of course, the Italy of that time did not enter into this alliance treaty to enable the German people to achieve national unity, but rather the Italian people. That requires the proverbial political naivety of a patriotic agitator to be able to see it as a cause for reproach or defamation. The notion of maintaining an alliance where only one party has prospects of success or gain from the outset is childish stupidity. For just as the Italians would have the right to accuse the Prussia of that time and Bismarck of the same reproach, namely, that it entered into the alliance not only out of love for Italy but also in pursuit of its own interests. Unfortunately, I would almost say it is shameful that this stupidity is only committed north of the Alps and not also south.

Such stupidity could only be understood when considering the Triple Alliance or, better yet, the alliance between Germany and Austria, namely, the truly rare case in which one state, namely Austria, had everything from the alliance and the other, namely Germany, had nothing. An alliance in which one party put forth its interests and the other its shining defense. One [rational purpose] cold pragmatism and the other unwavering loyalty. At least to such an extent and in this manner, there has only been one instance in world history, and Germany received the most terrible receipt for this type of political leadership and alliance policy. So, if the alliance with Italy, as far as Austria's relationship with Italy was concerned, was of dubious value from the beginning, it was not because Italy could be a fundamentally wrong partner, but because for Italy, this alliance with Austria promised not a single real equivalent.

Italy was a nation-state. Its future inevitably lay on the shores of the Mediterranean Sea. Each neighboring state was thus more or less an obstacle to the development of this nation-state.

Adding to this, Austria itself had over 800,000 Italians within its borders, and conversely, the same Habsburgs who, on the one hand, subjected the Germans to Czechization, on the other, understood very well how to pit Slavs and Germans against Italians, had every interest in slowly denationalizing these 800,000 Italians. Therefore, the future task of Italian foreign policy was hardly doubtful. As friendly as it could be towards Germany, it had to be hostile towards Austria. And this policy found the most lively support, indeed fervent enthusiasm, among the Italian people themselves.

For from the Italian standpoint, what the Habsburgs, with Austria as their political weapon, had done to Italy over the centuries was, viewed from an Italian perspective, outrageous. For centuries, Austria had been the obstacle to the unification of the Italian people; time and again, the Habsburgs had supported corrupt Italian dynasties. Indeed, around the turn of the century, hardly a congress of the clerical and Christian-social movement in Vienna ended without the call to return Rome to the Holy Father. They did not hide the fact that they saw this as a task of Austrian politics, but on the other hand, they had the audacity to expect bright enthusiasm from Italy itself for the alliance with Austria.

Throughout the centuries, Austrian policy towards Italy had by no means always used delicate gloves. What France had been for Germany for centuries, Austria had been for Italy for centuries. The northern Italian plain was repeatedly the battleground on which the Austrian state pursued its policy of friendship against Italy.

Croatian regiments and pandurs were the bearers of Austrian civilization, and it is a pity that this, to some extent, also stuck to the German name. If today one often hears from Italian mouths an arrogant underestimation, indeed contemptuous insult, of German culture, then the German people have to thank that state, which was disguised outwardly as German but revealed to Italians the nature of its inner being through a soldiery that was felt by those blessed with it in the Austrian state itself as a true scourge of God. The battle glory of the Austrian army was partly built on successes that had to evoke the eternal hatred of the Italian for all time.

It was a misfortune for Germany never to have realized this, a misfortune that, on the contrary, indirectly, if not directly, covered up. For in this way, Germany lost the state that, as things stood, could have been our most faithful ally, as it had once been a very reliable one for Prussia.

Particularly decisive for Italy's internal relationship with Austria was the attitude of the broadest public opinion in Austria during the Tripolitan War. It was understandable that in Vienna, there was a wary eye on Italian attempts to establish a foothold in Albania, as Austria believed its own interests were threatened there. However, what was incomprehensible was the general and decidedly artificially stoked agitation against Italy when it set out to acquire Tripolitania. The Italian step was a matter of course. No one could blame the Italian government for attempting to raise the Italian flag in areas that, by their very location, must have been given colonial territory for Italy.

Not only did young Italian colonizers encounter traces of ancient Roman history there, but Italian action would have been welcomed by Germany and Austria for another reason as well. The more Italy became involved in North Africa, the more natural conflicts had to develop between Italy and France. A superior German leadership, at least, should have sought to impede the threatening expansion of French hegemony over North Africa, and indeed the French exploitation of the black continent, considering the possible military strengthening of France on European battlefields. For the French governments, and especially their military leadership, left no doubt that for them, the African colonies had a significance other than being mere demonstration objects of French civilization.

For a long time, they had seen them as reservoirs of soldiers for the next European confrontation. Since this confrontation could only take place with Germany, it was also clear that every effort should be made from Germany to favor the intervention of any other power, especially if that power was a fellow ally. Additionally, the French populace was sterile and did not need to expand its living space, while the Italian people, like the Germans, had to find some outlet. It should not be said that this was a robbery of Turkey.

All colonies are thus territories acquired by theft, but Europeans cannot live without them. We had no interest in, and should not have possessed any, alienating Italy due to entirely unrealistic sympathetic feelings for Turkey. If ever in a foreign policy action, Austria and Germany could have completely supported Italy. However, the way the Austrian press, indeed the entire opinion, behaved towards Italian actions, which in the final analysis were nothing but the annexation of Bosnia and Herzegovina by Austria itself, was simply scandalous. At that time, a sudden hatred flared up that showed the real inner attitude of this Austro-Italian relationship all the more clearly, as there had been no actual reason for it. I myself was in Vienna at that time and was internally outraged by the foolish and impudent manner in which the ally was stabbed in the back.

Under such circumstances, demanding loyalty from this ally that would have been suicide for Italy is at least as incomprehensible as it is naive. Moreover, the natural military-geographical situation of Italy will always force this state to pursue a policy that does not bring it into conflict with an overpowering naval power, against which resistance by the Italian fleet and its allies would not be humanly foreseeable. As long as England maintains undisputed maritime supremacy and this hegemony can be strengthened by a Mediterranean French fleet without Italy and its allies being able to offer any viable resistance, Italy will never be able to adopt an anti-English stance.

However, one cannot expect a government to abandon itself to certain destruction out of blind sympathy for another state, whose reciprocal affection had been clearly demonstrated by the Tripolitan War. Anyone who takes even the most cursory look at the coastal conditions of the Italian state must readily come to the conclusion that a conflict between Italy and England under the prevailing circumstances is not only hopeless but absurd. Thus, Italy found itself in exactly the same situation as Germany, namely: just as for Bismarck, the risk of a war with Russia caused by Austria seemed so monstrous for Germany that he committed himself to disregard the otherwise given alliance case through the famous Reinsurance Treaty, so too was the alliance with Austria untenable for Italy at the moment it made England its enemy. Anyone who fails to understand or refuses to understand this is incapable of thinking politically and therefore at most capable of making politics in Germany. However, the result of the politics of these kinds of people lies before the German nation today, and it has to bear the consequences.

All these are points that must have reduced the value of the alliance with

Austria to a minimum. It was certain that, in addition to Russia, Romania, and Serbia, Germany would probably also gain Italy as an opponent for its alliance with Austria. As I mentioned, there is no alliance that could be built on ideal sympathies, loyalty, or gratitude.

Alliances will be stronger to the extent that each party can hope to gain personal advantages from them. Attempting to found an alliance on a different basis is fantastical. I will never expect Italy to enter into a federal relationship with Germany out of sympathy for Germany, love for Germany, and with the intention of benefiting Germany.

Similarly, I would never be able to enter into a contractual relationship out of love for another state, sympathy for it, or a desire to benefit it. If I advocate today for a federal relationship between Italy and Germany, it is only because I believe that both states can gain useful advantages from it. Both states will make good deals.

However, the benefit of the Triple Alliance lay exclusively on Austria's side. Already due to the determining factors in the policies of individual states, Austria could always be the beneficiary of this alliance. Because the Triple Alliance had no aggressive tendencies whatsoever.

It was a defensive alliance that, at the very least, was intended to secure the preservation of the status quo. Germany and Italy were forced by the impossibility of sustaining their population to pursue an offensive policy. Only Austria alone had to be content with keeping the already impossible state corpse alive.

Since Austria's own defensive power would never have been sufficient for this purpose, the offensive forces of Germany and Italy were harnessed in the service of Austrian state preservation by the Triple Alliance. Germany remained in harness and perished, while Italy jumped out and saved itself. It would only be possible for someone who does not consider politics as the obligation to preserve a people's existence by all means and according to all possibilities to want to raise a reproach against this. Even if old Germany as a formal nation-state had set the further unification of the German nation as its foreign policy goal, it had to immediately abandon the Triple Alliance or change its relationship with Austria. Countless enmities would have been spared as a result, which could not have been eliminated by Austria's exertion of force.

However, even the Germany of the pre-war period could no longer allow its foreign policy to be determined purely by formal national considerations if these did not lead to vitally necessary goals. Already in the pre-war period, the future of the German people was a question of solving the food problem. The German people could no longer find their daily bread within the available space.

All diligence, all efficiency, and all scientific methods in land cultivation could only alleviate this distress somewhat but could not definitively prevent it. Even in years of exceptionally good harvests, a complete coverage of the country's own food needs was no longer possible. In the case of average or even poor harvests, a very considerable percentage had to rely on imports. The supply of raw materials for some industries also encountered serious difficulties and could only be obtained from abroad.

The ways to alleviate this distress could be various. Emigration and birth control had to be categorically rejected even from the standpoint of the then-existing nation-state, where the fear of numerical decimation became determinative rather than the recognition of biological consequences. Thus, for Germany at that time, there could actually only be two possibilities to ensure the preservation of the nation for the foreseeable future without having to restrict the population itself. Either one attempted to alleviate the lack of space by acquiring new land or one transformed the empire into a large exporting company. That is, one increased the production of certain goods beyond the scope of domestic demand, in order to then exchange food and raw materials through exports.

The recognition of the necessity for an expansion of German living space was, at least partially, present at that time. It was believed that the best course of action in line with this recognition was to integrate Germany into the ranks of the great colonial powers. However, in reality, there was already a breach of internal logic due to the form in which this idea was implemented.

The essence of sound land policy lies in expanding a nation's living space by allocating new territories for settlement to the surplus of the population, which must, however, be in close political and state relationship with the motherland if it is not to take on the character of emigration. This was no longer the case with the colonies that were still tangible at the end of the 19th century.

Neither the geographical distance nor the climatic conditions of these areas allowed for settlement, as the English had been able to do in their American colonies, the Dutch in South Africa, and again the English in Australia. Furthermore, the entire nature of German colonial policy placed the settlement problem completely in the background, substituting it with societal interests that were only minimally aligned with general German national interests. Thus, from the outset, the value of the German colonies lay more in the possibility of securing certain markets, which would make the German economy independent from abroad by providing various colonial products and partly raw materials.

To a certain extent, this would have been successful in the future as well, but it would not have solved Germany's overpopulation problem in the slightest, unless one decided to guarantee the German people's sustenance fundamentally by increasing its export economy. Then, of course, the German colonies could one day provide greater competitiveness on the international markets by supplying various industries with raw materials more favorably. However, German colonial policy, in its deepest essence, was thus not land policy but rather a tool for German economic policy. Indeed, the direct numerical relief of the German domestic overpopulation through colonization of the colonies was completely insignificant.

Moreover, if one wanted to transition to a real space policy, then the colonial policy pursued before the war was all the more nonsensical, as it could lead to a tangible relief of the German overpopulation, but conversely would one day, according to all human foresight, require the same bloodshed for its implementation as would have been necessary in the worst case for a truly useful space policy. For, while this type of German colonial policy could only bring a strengthening of the German economy at best, it had to one day become a cause for brutal confrontation with England. Because a German world economic policy could never avoid the decisive struggle with England.

Export industry, world trade, colonies, and merchant fleet would then have to be defended with the sword against that power, which, out of the same self-preservation motives as Germany, had long before felt compelled to embark on this path. Therefore, as long as England could count on bringing about the collapse of German competition with purely economic means, this economic peaceful struggle for the conquest of a place in the sun could take place because we never emerged from the shadow. But if Germany succeeded in pushing back England on this economically peaceful path, then it was natural that the phantom of this economically peaceful world conquest would be replaced by resistance of bayonets.

Without a doubt, it was nonetheless a political idea to allow the German people to increase their numbers through the expansion of their industrial productions and their sales on the international world market. This idea was not ethnic in nature, but it corresponded to the concepts of the bourgeois-national world prevailing at that time. In any case, this path prescribed a very specific obligation for German foreign policy: the end of German world trade policy could only be the war with England. Then, however, German foreign policy had the task of preparing for confrontation with a state that, based on several hundred years of experience, would spare no effort to bring about a general mobilization of allied states.

If Germany wanted to defend its industrial and economic policy against England, it had to seek its first support from Russia. Russia was then the only state that could be considered a valuable ally, because it alone did not necessarily have any significant contradictions with Germany, at least for the moment. However, the price for this Russian alliance could, given the circumstances, only lie in the abandonment of the alliance with Austria. For then the Dual Alliance with Austria was madness, indeed insanity.

Only if Germany had full support from Russia could it transition to a maritime policy consciously aimed at the day of reckoning. Then it could also most promptly employ the enormous resources necessary for the expansion of a fleet, which, not constructively in everything, but especially in speed and thus displacement, lagged behind five years. However, the entanglement in the Austrian alliance was so great that a solution could no longer be found, and consequently Russia, which began to reorient itself after the Russo-Japanese War, had to be definitively repelled. But then the entire German economic and colonial policy became more than a dangerous game.

The fact was that Germany also shied away from the final confrontation with England and accordingly allowed its behavior to be determined by the principle of not provoking the opponent for years. This principle governed all German decisions that would have been necessary to protect German economic and colonial policy until August 4, 1914, when the English declaration of war ended this period of unfortunate German delusion. If the Germany of that time had been less dominated by bourgeois-national than by ethnic considerations, only the other path of a solution to German distress would have been possible, namely that of a generous space policy in Europe itself.

The German colonial policy, which necessarily had to bring us into conflict with England, with France always being able to be considered on the side of the opponents, was particularly unreasonable for Germany because our European base was weaker than that of any other colonial people of world political significance. Because finally, the fate of the colonies in Europe was decided. Consequently, every German foreign policy was dependent on consolidating and securing Germany's military position in Europe in the first place. We could expect very little decisive help from our colonies in this regard.

Conversely, any expansion of our European territorial base would have naturally led to a strengthening of our position. It is not the same whether a people possess a contiguous settlement area of 560,000 or say 1 million square kilometers. Quite apart from the difficulty of sustenance in case of war, which should remain as independent as possible from the influence of the opponent, there is already a military protection in the size of the spatial area itself, insofar as our operations that force us to wage war on our own soil are substantially easier to bear.

Moreover, there is already a certain protection against reckless attacks in the size of a state's territory.

Above all, only through a space policy in Europe could the human capital deported there remain preserved for our people, up to and including military utilization. An additional 500,000 square kilometers of land in Europe could offer millions of German farmers new homesteads, but for the decisive moment, it could provide millions of soldiers to the German nation.

The only area in Europe suitable for such a land policy was then Russia. The sparsely populated western border regions adjacent to Germany, which had once received German colonizers as bearers of culture, were also suitable for the new European land policy of the German nation. Then the goal of German foreign policy must absolutely be to free itself from England and, conversely, to isolate Russia as much as possible. Then, with ruthless consistency, our economic and world trade policy had to be abandoned, if necessary, completely giving up the fleet to concentrate the entire nation's strength back on the army, as it once was.

But then, all the more, the alliance with Austria had to be abandoned, because nothing stood in the way of isolating Russia more than the protection provided by Germany to a state whose division was desired by a whole number of European powers, but could only have been carried out in alliance with Russia. However, since these states had recognized in Germany the most powerful protection for the preservation of Austria, they had to be even more against the isolation of Russia, as to them, the Tsarist Empire could then appear as the only possible force for the final destruction of Austria.

But that all these states could not wish for a strengthening of the only support for Austria at the expense of the strongest opponent of the Habsburg state is obvious. Since in this case, too, France would always have stood on the side of Germany's opponents, the possibility of a coalition against Germany would always have been present if one did not decide to at least definitively liquidate the alliance with Austria around the turn of the century, leaving the Austrian state to its fate but saving the German lands for the Reich.

It turned out differently. Germany wanted world peace. It therefore avoided a land policy that could only have been fought aggressively and finally turned to an endless economic and trade policy. It sought to conquer the world with economic peaceful means, relying on neither one nor the other power.

As a result, as a general political isolation set in, it clung ever more desperately to the dying Habsburg state. Large segments within Germany welcomed this, partly out of genuine political incapacity, out of misunderstood patriotic-legitimist trains of thought, and finally also in the secretly nurtured hope that by doing so, the hated Hohenzollern imperial reign could one day be brought to collapse.

When the World War erupted in blood-red on August 2, 1914, the alliance policy of the pre-war period had already received its actual defeat. Germany had been forced into a fight to help Austria, which then turned into a struggle for its own existence. Its enemies were the adversaries of its world trade and its general greatness, as well as the contenders for Austria's dissolution.

Its friends were the most improbable state entity, Austria-Hungary, on one side, and the perpetually ailing and weak Turkey on the other. However, Italy took the step that Germany would have had to take, and would have taken, if the genius of a Bismarck had guided its destiny instead of feeble philosophers and brawling cheer-patriots. That it later launched an offensive against a former ally again only corresponds to that prophetic foresight of Bismarck, that there could only be two states between Italy and Austria: alliance or war.

---------------------------------- 19 ----------------------------------

CHAPTER 8
The Necessity of Military Power

---------------------------------- 28 ----------------------------------

On November 11, 1918, the armistice was signed in the forest of Compiègne. Fate had designated a man as one of the primary culprits in the collapse of our nation. Matthias Erzberger, a member of the Centre Party and, according to various claims, the illegitimate son of a maid and a Jewish master, was the German negotiator who also placed his name on a document that, when compared and measured against the four and a half years of our people's heroic era, seems incomprehensible unless one accepts the deliberate intention to destroy Germany.

Matthias Erzberger himself had been a minor bourgeois politician favoring annexation, thus one of those men who, particularly at the start of the war, had tried to compensate for the lack of an official war goal in their own way. Even though in August 1914, the entire German nation instinctively felt that this conflict was about survival or extinction, there was no clear understanding, as the flames of initial enthusiasm died down, of the looming extinction or the necessary survival. The magnitude of the idea of defeat and its consequences were slowly erased by propaganda, which had free rein inside Germany and which twisted or completely denied the real war aims of the Entente in as cunning as it was deceitful a manner. In the second and especially in the third year of the war, it was already successful in removing the German people's fear of defeat to the extent that they no longer believed in the magnitude of the enemy's intent on annihilation, thanks to this propaganda. This was all the more terrible as, conversely, nothing could be done to inform the people of what needed to be achieved at a minimum for their future self-preservation and as a reward for their extraordinary sacrifices.

The discussion about a possible war goal, therefore, took place only within more or less irresponsible circles and now also represented the mindset and general political views of their respective representatives. While clever Marxism, well aware of the paralyzing effect of the lack of a specific war aim, categorically forbade such an aim and otherwise only spoke of restoring peace without annexations and reparations, at least part of the bourgeois politicians tried to counter the magnitude of the bloodshed and the outrage of the assault with specific counter-demands. All these bourgeois suggestions were mere border adjustments and had nothing to do with spatial-political thoughts. At most, they considered fulfilling the expectations of certain currently unemployed German princes by creating buffer states, and thus, with few exceptions, even the establishment of the Polish State appeared to the bourgeois world as a politically wise decision. Some pushed economic considerations to the forefront, according to which the border should be shaped, e.g., the necessity of acquiring the Longwy and Briey ore basins, others again expressed strategic opinions, e.g., the necessity of obtaining control over the Belgian Meuse fortifications, etc.

That this was no goal for a war of a nation against 26, in which it had to undertake the most colossal bloodshed in history while back home an entire people were literally left to starve, should have been self-evident. The impossibility of justifying the need to continue the war based on these grounds contributed to its unfortunate outcome.

Thus, when the collapse of the homeland occurred, knowledge of war aims was even less present, as their previously feeble proponents had since distanced themselves even from the few demands they once made. And this was actually understandable. To want to conduct a war of these unprecedented proportions so that the border would run over Liège instead of Herbesthal, or so that instead of a Tsarist commissioner or governor over some Russian province, a German little prince is installed as a potentate, would really be irresponsible and sacrilegious. It was in the nature of the German war aims, as far as they were discussed at all, that they were later all denied. Because indeed, for such trivialities, one really could not keep a nation in a war for even an hour longer, whose battlefields had slowly become hell.

The only war aim worthy of this immense bloodshed could have only consisted of assuring the German soldiers that so many 100,000 square kilometers of land would be assigned to the front fighters as property, or made available for general colonization by Germans. This would have also immediately stripped the war of the character of an imperial enterprise and turned it instead into a matter of the German people. After all, the German grenadiers truly did not shed their blood so that the Poles could have a state or so that a German prince could be placed on a plush throne.

In 1918, this marked the end of a completely senseless and aimless squandering of the most precious German blood.

Once again, our people had invested immensely in heroism, willingness to sacrifice, indeed courage in the face of death, and a spirit of responsibility, and yet had to leave the battlefield beaten and weakened. Victorious in a thousand battles and skirmishes and in the end defeated by those who were beaten. A portent for German domestic and foreign policy of the pre-war period and the 4 1/2 years of bloody struggle itself.

Now, after the collapse, the anxious question arises whether our German people have learned anything from this catastrophe, whether those who have consciously betrayed it until now will continue to determine its fate, whether those who have already failed so miserably with their phrases will continue to dominate the future, or whether finally, in terms of domestic and foreign policy, our people will be educated to a new way of thinking and accordingly adjust their actions.

For if a miracle does not occur with our people, their path will be one of ultimate ruin.

What is the current situation of Germany, and what are the prospects for its future, and what will this future be like?

The collapse that the German people suffered in 1918, as I want to reaffirm here, does not lie in the downfall of its military organization or the loss of its weapons but in the internal decay revealed at that time and becoming increasingly apparent today. This internal decay is as much about the deterioration of its racial value as it is about the loss of all those virtues that determine the greatness of a nation, ensure its existence, and promote its future.

The value of blood, the concept of individuality, and the instinct for self-preservation are slowly disappearing from the German people. Instead, internationalism triumphs and destroys our national values, democracy spreads by stabbing the concept of individuality, and finally, a vile pacifist sludge poisons the mindset of bold self-preservation. We see the effects of these vices of humanity manifesting throughout the entire life of our people. Not only in the realm of political concerns but also in those of the economy and, not least, in our cultural life, a downward slide is noticeable, which, if not halted, will exclude our people from the ranks of nations with a promising future.

The great domestic political task of the future lies in the elimination of these general signs of decay in our people. This is the mission of the National Socialist movement. From this work, a new national body must emerge that also overcomes the worst damage of the present, the class division, for which the bourgeoisie and Marxism are equally to blame.

However, the goal of this reformation work of domestic politics must ultimately be the regaining of our people's strength to carry out their struggle for existence and thus the power to represent their interests abroad.

As a result, our foreign policy is also assigned the task it has to fulfill. For as much as domestic policy must provide the national instrument of power to foreign policy, so too must foreign policy through its actions and measures promote and support the formation of this instrument.

If the task of the foreign policy of the old bourgeois-national state initially had been the further unification of the members of the German nation in Europe, to then ascend to a higher, racially perceived spatial policy, then the task of post-war foreign policy must first be one of promoting the internal instrument of power. Because the foreign policy aspirations of the pre-war era were supported by a state that, although not very highly regarded in national terms, had a wonderful military setup available. Even though the Germany of that era no longer had such an emphasis on the military as, for example, the old Prussia, and therefore was surpassed by other states particularly in terms of the extent of military organization, the inner quality of the old army was incomparably superior to all similar institutions. This best instrument of the art of war was available to a bold foreign policy leadership at that time. Because of this instrument and the general respect it enjoyed, the freedom of our people was not just a matter [an affair] of our actually proven strength, but also of the general credit we had due to this unique military instrument and also partly due to the rest of the exemplary clean state apparatus.

Today, the German people no longer possess this most important instrument for the protection of a people's interests, or at least not to a sufficient extent and far removed from the foundation that conditioned its former strength.

The German people have acquired a mercenary army. This mercenary force is in danger of degenerating into a police force equipped with special technical weapons in Germany. The comparison between the German mercenary army and the English one turns out unfavorably for the Germans. The English mercenary army has always been the bearer of the military defense and offensive ideas as well as the military tradition of England. England had in its mercenary troop and its unique militia system the army organization that, given its insular position, sufficed for the defense of English life interests and seemed appropriate. The idea that allowed the English resistance to express itself in such a form was by no means born out of cowardice to spare the general bloodshed of the English people. On the contrary, England fought with mercenaries as long as the mercenaries sufficed for the defense of English interests. It called for volunteers as soon as the conflict required a larger commitment. It introduced conscription as soon as the nation's need dictated it. Because no matter what the current organization of English resistance was like, it was always used for the relentless fight for England. And the formal military organization in England was always just an instrument for the defense of English interests, employed by a will that did not shy away from, if necessary, demanding the blood of the entire nation. Where England's interests were crucially at stake, it knew how to maintain a supremacy that, technically speaking, extends to the demand for a two-power standard.

If one compares the infinite [concerned] responsible concern involved with the recklessness with which Germany, specifically the national bourgeois Germany, neglected its armament in the pre-war period, one must still be deeply saddened today. Just as England knew that its future, indeed its very existence, depended on the strength of its navy, the bourgeois national Germany should have known that the existence and future of the German Empire depended on the strength of our land forces. Germany should have countered the maritime two-power standard in Europe with a land-based two-power standard. And just as England saw in any violation of this standard a cause for war with iron determination, Germany in Europe had to prevent any attempt by France and Russia to outpace its armed forces with a military decision that had to be initiated by Germany itself and for which more than one favorable opportunity had presented itself. In this respect, the bourgeoisie has misused a Bismarckian phrase in the most senseless way. The statement by Bismarck that he had no intention of waging a preventive war was eagerly seized by all weak, energy-less, and irresponsible politicians to cover their policy of letting things happen, which must have devastating consequences. They completely forgot that all three wars that Bismarck waged were, at least according to the views of these anti-preventive war peace philosophers, avoidable.

Think what, for example, the German Republic of today would have had to suffer in terms of insults from Napoleon III in 1870 for it to decide to ask Mr. Benedetti to moderate his tone. Neither Napoleon nor the entire French nation could ever have provoked the German Republic of today into a Sedan. Or does one believe that the war of 1866, had Bismarck not desired the decision, could not have been avoided? However, one might argue that these were wars to achieve clearly defined goals and not ones based on the fear of an attack by the opponent. But in reality, this is just quibbling. Because Bismarck was convinced that a conflict with Austria was inevitable, he prepared for it and fought it under circumstances favorable to Prussia. The French military reform by Marshal Niel clearly indicated the intention to provide French politics and French chauvinism with the powerful weapon to attack Germany.

Indeed, Bismarck would have undoubtedly been able to settle the conflict in 1870 peacefully in some manner. However, it was more appropriate to fight it at a time when the French military organization had not yet reached full effectiveness. Moreover, all these interpretations of Bismarck's statements suffer from one thing: they confuse the diplomat Bismarck with a republican parliamentarian. The best indication of how Bismarck himself judged such statements is his response to a questioner before the outbreak of the Prussian-Austrian war, who wanted to know if Bismarck really intended to attack Austria, to which he replied with an inscrutable face: No, I have no intention of attacking Austria, but I would also not have the intention, if I wanted to attack them, to tell them.

Moreover, the severest war ever fought by Prussia was a preventive war. When Frederick the Great finally learned of the intentions of his old adversaries through a clerk's soul, he did not wait out of a fundamental objection to a preventive war for the others to attack; he himself immediately went on the offensive.

Every violation of the two-power standard should have been a cause for a preventive war for Germany. For what would have been easier to justify before history, a preventive war that would have defeated France in 1904 when Russia was bound in East Asia, or the resulting World War that required multiples more bloodshed and plunged our nation into the deepest defeat. England never had such reservations. Its two-power standard at sea seemed to be the prerequisite for the preservation of English independence. As long as it had the strength, it allowed no change to this state. However, if this two-power standard was abandoned after the World War, it was only under the pressure of circumstances that were stronger than any opposing English intention. In the American Union, a new power factor has emerged of dimensions that threatens to overthrow the entire previous power and ranking orders of the states.

In any case, the English fleet has always been the most striking proof that, regardless of the form of the organization of the land army, the will to preserve England determined decisively. Therefore, the English mercenary army never acquired the bad qualities of other mercenary troops. It was a fighting and brawling bunch with wonderful individual training, excellent equipment, and a sportingly perceived understanding of service. What gave this small army corps special significance was its direct contact with the visible manifestations of life of the British Empire. This mercenary army fought for England's greatness in almost all parts of the world as much as it learned of England's greatness. The men who represented England's interests in South Africa, Egypt, and India as bearers of its military esteem also received indelible impressions of the immense size of the British Empire.

This possibility is completely lacking in the current German mercenary force. Yes, the more one feels compelled, under the impression of pacifist-democratic, in reality nationally and traitorously democratic parliamentary majorities, to make concessions to this spirit in the small army itself, the more it also ceases to be an instrument of war, instead becoming a police force for maintaining peace and order, which in reality means peaceful submission. One cannot train an army of high intrinsic value if its existence's purpose is not the preparation for war. There are no armies for maintaining peace, only for victoriously conducting war. The more Germany tries to lift the Reichswehr out of the tradition of the old army, the more it becomes traditionless. Because the traditional value of a troop lies not in a few successful suppressions of internal strike revolts or in preventing looting of food supplies, but in the glory of victorious battles won.

The German Reichswehr is actually moving away from the tradition of this glory each year more as it ceases to be a representative of the national thought. The more it finally kills the consciously national, that is, nationalist spirit within its own ranks and removes its representatives to instead give positions to democrats and ordinary careerists, the more it becomes alien to the people. For the cunning gentlemen should not delude themselves that by making concessions to the pacifist-democratic part of our people, they will connect with the people. This part of the German people inherently despises any military organization as long as it remains military and not a guard and security company for international-pacifist stock exchange interests. The only part with which an army can have an inner relationship in a militarily valuable sense is that nationally conscious core of our people, which not only thinks militarily out of tradition but also, out of national love, is the only one willing to don the gray coat to protect honor and freedom. It is necessary that a military body maintains internal relations with those from whom it can replenish itself in times of need and not with those who would betray it at every opportunity. Hence, today's leaders of our so-called Reichswehr can act as democratically as they want, but they will never be able to connect more closely with the German people, because the part of the German people suitable for this is not found in the camp of democracy. However, especially the former head of the German Reichswehr, General von Seeckt, by not only offering no resistance to the removal of gnarled, consciously national-minded officers but even advocating it, ultimately created the instrument that then allowed him to depart relatively easily.

Since the resignation of General von Seeckt, the democratic-pacifist influence has been tirelessly active in turning the German Reichswehr into what the rulers of today's state envisage as the ideal: a republican-democratic parliamentary guard. However, such an instrument is naturally not suitable for conducting foreign policy. Therefore, the immediate task of German domestic policy today should be to provide the German people with an appropriate military organization of their national strength. Since the forms of the current Reichswehr can never suffice for this purpose and are, conversely, determined by external political factors, it is the task of German foreign policy to bring about all possibilities that would allow for the reorganization of a German national army. For it must be the unshakeable goal of every political leadership in Germany that one day the mercenary army will be replaced by a true German national army.

As poor as the general qualities of the German Reichswehr must develop in the future, the purely technical-military qualities of the present are outstanding. This is undoubtedly the merit of General von Seeckt and the Reichswehr officer corps in general. In this way, the German Reichswehr could indeed be the framework army for the coming German national army. After all, the task of the Reichswehr itself should be, with an educational emphasis on the national combat mission, to train the mass of [future] officers and sergeants for the later national army.

That this goal must be kept in view as an immovable one, no true nationally minded German can dispute. Just as undeniable, however, is that its implementation will only be possible if the nation's foreign policy leadership secures the generally necessary prerequisites.

Thus, the first task of German foreign policy is to create conditions that enable the re-establishment of a German army. For only then will the vital needs of our people be able to find their practical representation. It should be noted, fundamentally, that the political actions meant to ensure the re-emergence of a German army must lie within the framework of the future development necessary for Germany itself.

It goes without saying that a change in the current military organization, apart from the current domestic political situation, cannot take place for external political reasons as long as only German interests and viewpoints speak for such a change.

It was in the nature of the World War and in the intention of Germany's main enemies to carry out the liquidation of this greatest combat operation on earth in such a way that as many states as possible are interested in its perpetuation. This was achieved by creating a system of land distributions that kept even states with otherwise very diverging wishes and goals united in opposition through the fear of suffering losses in case of a resurgence of Germany. For if it is still possible, 10 years after the end of the World War, contrary to all previous experiences of world history, to maintain a kind of coalition of victorious states, then the reason lies only in the truly glorious fact for Germany of the reminiscence of that struggle, in which our fatherland faced 26 states.

This will remain the case as long as the fear of incurring losses through a re-emerging German power is greater than the difficulties these states have among each other. And it is further self-evident that as long as this is the case, there is also nowhere a will to permit the German people to arm themselves in a way that could then be perceived as a threat by these victorious states. However, from the realization that, firstly, a true representation of German life interests in the future can only occur not through an insufficient German Reichswehr but only through a German national army; secondly, the formation of a German national army is impossible as long as the current external political strangulation of Germany does not ease; and thirdly, a change in the external political resistance against the organization of a national army seems possible only if such a new formation is not universally perceived as a threat, it follows for the currently possible German foreign policy this fact:

Modern Germany must under no circumstances see its foreign policy task in a formal border policy. As soon as the principle of restoring the borders of 1914 is established as a foreign policy objective, Germany will face a united phalanx of its former enemies. This then eliminates any possibility of changing the form of our army determined by the peace treaty to another form that serves our interests better. Thus, the foreign policy slogan: Restoration of the borders, has become a mere phrase because it can never be realized due to the lack of necessary power.

It is characteristic that precisely the so-called German bourgeoisie, and here again at the forefront the patriotic associations, have taken up this most foolish foreign policy objective. They know that Germany is powerless. They further know that, apart from our internal decay, military means would be necessary to restore our borders; they know further that we do not possess these means due to the peace treaties and that we cannot obtain them due to the united front of our opponents; [they know further that we cannot regain the borders of 1914] but they still set forth a foreign policy slogan that just by its very nature forever removes the possibility for us to come to those means of power necessary for its implementation.

Such is then called bourgeois statecraft and indeed shows by the fruits we see before us the unparalleled spirit that governs it.

Seven years were enough for the then Prussia from 1806 to 1813 for its resurgence. [And in 10 years] In the same time, bourgeois statecraft in union with Marxism has led Germany up to Locarno. What then, in the eyes of today's bourgeois Bismarck, Mr. Stresemann, is a great success because it represents the possible, what the said Mr. Stresemann could achieve. And politics is the art of the possible. If Bismarck ever had suspected that he is doomed by fate to confirm the statesmanlike qualities of Mr. Stresemann with this statement, he would have either surely refrained from making it or would have excluded Mr. Stresemann in a brief remark from the right to refer to it.

The slogan of the restoration of German borders as a foreign policy objective for the future is doubly foolish and dangerous because it in reality does not encompass any useful and desirable goal whatsoever.

The German borders of the year 1914 represented something incomplete, just as the borders of peoples have been at all times. The distribution of space on Earth at any time is the immediate result of a struggle and development, which is by no means concluded but naturally continues. To take the border of any specific year from the history of a people and summarily present it as a political goal is foolish. Just as well as one could establish the border of the year 1914, one could choose the border of the year 1648 or of 1312, etc. This is all the more true as the border of the year 1914 was neither nationally, militarily, nor geopolitically satisfactory in any way. It was just the momentary state at that time in the life struggle of our people, which has been unfolding for millennia and even if the World War had not occurred, would not have found its termination in 1914.

If the German people were actually to achieve the restoration of the borders of 1914, nevertheless, the sacrifices of the World War would have been in vain. But also, the future of our people would not gain the slightest by such a restoration. This purely formal border policy of our national bourgeoisie is just as unsatisfactory in potential result as it is unbearably dangerous. It must not even refer to the saying of the art of the possible, for it is only a theoretical phrase that seems suitable to destroy every practical possibility.

In fact, such a foreign policy objective cannot withstand a truly critical examination. Therefore, it is also less sought to be motivated by logical reasons than by reasons of national honor.

National honor demands that we restore the borders of 1914. That is so the tenor of the arguments at the beer evenings that the representatives of national honor organize everywhere.

National honor initially has nothing to do with an obligation to pursue a foolish and impossible foreign policy. Because the result of a poor foreign policy can be the loss of a people's freedom, whose consequence then is enslavement, which certainly cannot be considered a state of national honor. Of course, even under oppression, a certain degree of national dignity and honor can be maintained, but this is then not a matter of shouting or national phrases, etc., but on the contrary, the expression of the decency of a people is to be found in the way this people bears its fate.

In today's Germany, do not speak of national honor, and do not try to create the impression that by any kind of rhetorical barking to the outside world, national honor can be preserved. No, it cannot be preserved, primarily because it is no longer there. And it is not missing because we lost the war or because the French occupied Alsace-Lorraine, the Poles took Upper Silesia, or the Italians took South Tyrol.

No, the national honor is gone because, during the most challenging time of its struggle for survival, the German people showed a lack of conviction, shameless subservience, and a doggishly crawling sycophancy that can only be called shameless. Because we have miserably surrendered without being forced to, yes, because the leadership of this people, contrary to eternal historical truth and their own knowledge, has accepted the war guilt, indeed, burdened our entire nation with it, because there was no oppression by the opponents that did not find thousands of willing helpers within our own people. Because, conversely, they shamelessly vilified the time of the greatest deeds of our people, spat on the most glorious flag of all times, yes, sullied it with mud, tore off the honorable cockades from returning soldiers, before whom a world had trembled, threw dung at the flag, tore off medals and decorations, and dishonored the memory of Germany's greatest era a thousandfold.

No enemy has insulted the German army as much as it was sullied by the representatives of the November treachery. No foe has disputed the greatness of German military leaders as much as they were slandered by the ragged representatives of the new state idea. And what was more dishonorable for our people, the occupation of German territories by enemies, or the cowardice with which our bourgeoisie handed over the German Empire to an organization of pimps, street thieves, deserters, profiteers, and low-grade journalists. These gentlemen should now not prattle about German honor as long as they bow under the rule of dishonor. One has no right to conduct foreign policy in the name of national honor when domestic policy is the most anti-national shamelessness that has ever afflicted a great people.

Anyone who wants to act today in the name of German honor must first declare the most merciless fight against the infernal defilers of German honor. But these are not the former enemies, but the representatives of the November crime. That collection of Marxist, democratic-pacifist, and centralist traitors who have thrust our people into the state of its current impotence.

To rail against the enemies of the past in the name of national honor and to recognize the dishonorable allies of these enemies within as lords corresponds to the national dignity of this so-called national bourgeoisie of today.

I confess most openly that I could reconcile with every one of the former enemies, but my hatred against the traitors of our own people remains unrelenting.

What the enemies did to us is severe and deeply shameful for us, but what the men of the November crime have sinned is the most dishonorable, despicable crime of all times. By striving to create a state that will one day hold these creatures accountable, I am helping to repair German honor.

However, I must reject that the establishment of German foreign policy could be influenced by any other reasons than the responsibility to secure our people's freedom and future life.

The complete absurdity of the patriotic-bourgeois-national border policy arises from the following consideration:

The German nation counts, if the confession to the German mother tongue is the basis, ... million people.

[Of them, there are in the motherland . . . . million.

In that] .

———— 19 ————

CHAPTER 9
Neither Border Policy Nor Economic Policy nor Pan-Europe

———— 28 ————

Thus, within the current territory of the Reich, out of all Germans in the world, only . . . . million, which is . . . . percent of the total number of our people altogether.

Among the Germans not united with the motherland, those regarded as fellow countrymen destined for slow loss due to circumstances are . . . . , i.e., an estimated total of . . . . . . million Germans find themselves in a situation that, in all human probability, will eventually lead to their de-Germanization.

Under no circumstances, however, will they be able to continue participating in the motherland's struggle in any significant form, nor will they be able to contribute to the cultural development of their people. Whatever contribution German heritage makes in North America, it will not be credited to the German people themselves but will rather accrue to the cultural mass of the American Union. Here, Germans are truly only the cultural fertilizer for other peoples. Indeed, in reality, the greatness of these peoples is often attributed to German contributions to a high percentage overall.

When one considers the magnitude of these established losses of population, the limited significance of border policies protected by the bourgeois world becomes immediately apparent.

If German foreign policy were to restore the borders of 1914, the percentage of Germans living within the territory of the Reich, as members of our nation, would still only have increased from . . . . percent to . . . . percent. Any possibility of substantially increasing this percentage would hardly be feasible.

If German heritage abroad nevertheless wishes to remain loyal to the nation, it can initially only be a matter of linguistic and cultural loyalty, which will increasingly manifest as a consciously demonstrated sense of belonging, the more the motherland of the German nation, in the dignity of its representation of our people, honors the German name.

Thus, the more Germany itself, as the Reich of the world, conveys an impression of the greatness of the German people, the more incentive the German heritage definitively lost to the state will receive to at least spiritually boast its belonging to this people. Conversely, the more pitifully the motherland itself perceives the interests of the German nation and accordingly gives a poor impression outwardly, the weaker the internal motivation will be felt to belong to such a people.

But since the German people do not consist of Jews, especially in Anglo-Saxon countries, they will unfortunately continue to Anglicize more and more, and presumably also spiritually and intellectually become lost to our people just as their practical work output has already been lost to our people.

Regarding the fate of those Germans who were detached from the German body politic by the events of the World War and the peace treaties, it must be said that their fate and their future are a question of the political reconquest of the power of the motherland.

Lost territories are not recovered through protest actions, but through a victorious sword. And so, whoever today wishes for the liberation of any territory in the name of national honor must also be prepared to stand up with iron and blood for this liberation; otherwise, such a chatterer should keep their mouth shut. This then entails the duty to also weigh up, firstly, whether one even possesses the power to carry out such a fight, and secondly, whether the investment of blood can lead to the desired success and can be achieved, and thirdly, whether the achieved success corresponds to the investment of blood.

I solemnly protest against the notion that there could be an obligation of national honor to be forced to let two million men bleed to death on the battlefield, to then count as the most favorable result a quarter of a million men, women, and children combined. This is not national honor that appears here, but rather, it is recklessness or madness. However, for a people, it is no national honor to be ruled by lunatics.

Certainly, a people of greatness will shield even its last citizen with the commitment of its entirety. However, it is a mistake to attribute this to a feeling or honor, but rather, initially to an understanding of prudence and human experience. Just as a people would allow individual citizens to be wronged, it would slowly weaken its own position more and more, as such tolerance would serve as much to strengthen an aggressor as to erode confidence in the power of one's own state.

History is too familiar with the consequences of persistent leniency in small matters not to be able to judge the necessary consequences in larger matters. Therefore, a concerned government will prefer to safeguard the interests of its citizens even in the smallest matters, as the risk of its own commitment decreases in proportion to the increase in the opponent's. If today an individual belonging to England suffers injustice in any state, and England assumes the protection of its citizen, the risk of being drawn into war because of this single Englishman is no greater for England than for the other state inflicting the injustice. Hence, the firm stance of a respected state to protect even a single person is by no means an unbearable risk, as the other state will also have little interest in allowing a war to occur due to the triviality inflicted on a single person. From this realization and the thousand-year application of this principle, namely, that a powerful state protects and defends each of its citizens with its entire might, a general concept of honor has developed.

Furthermore, facilitated by the nature of European hegemony, over time, a certain practice has emerged to demonstrate this concept of honor through more or less inexpensive examples, to thereby bestow an increase or at least a continuity of respect upon individual European states in this manner. Whenever a Frenchman or Englishman in certain weak and militarily powerless countries suffered often either perceived or feigned injustice, then the protection of these subjects began to be taken over by force of arms. That is, a few warships staged a military demonstration, which in the worst case was live firing exercises, or some expeditionary force was landed, with which the offending power was then disciplined. Often, the desire to find any pretext for intervention was the inspiration for these actions. It is unlikely that the English would ever consider exchanging diplomatic notes with North America over a trivial matter that they bloody revenge in Liberia.

Therefore, as much as the protection of individual citizens will be assumed by a strong state for purely pragmatic reasons, it cannot be expected of a completely defenseless, powerless empire to undertake foreign policy measures for the sake of national honor that must inevitably lead to the destruction of any remaining prospects for the future. For if the German people justify their current border policy, advocated in so-called national circles, with the necessity of representing German honor, then the result will not be the restoration of German honor but rather the perpetuation of German dishonor. It is indeed not dishonorable to have lost territories, but it is dishonorable to pursue a policy that inevitably leads to the complete enslavement of one's own people.

And all of this just to indulge in vile rhetoric and avoid taking action. Because it is precisely that, mere rhetoric. If one truly wanted to pursue a policy of national honor, then one would at least entrust this policy to individuals who could be esteemed according to universal standards of honor.

However, as long as the internal and external policies of the German Reich are managed by forces that cynically declare in the German Reichstag that they have no fatherland called Germany, then it is primarily the task of these national bourgeois and patriotic phrase-mongers to first establish the most basic validity of the idea of national honor in Germany through their domestic policy. But why do they not do this? Why, on the contrary, do they form coalitions with declared traitors to the country at the expense of this so-called national honor? Because in the other case, a severe struggle would be necessary, the outcome of which they have little confidence in, and which might even lead to the destruction of their existence. However, their own private existence is then more sacred to them than defending national honor internally. Yet they are willing to gamble the future existence of the entire nation for the sake of a few phrases.

Moreover, national border policy becomes even more nonsensical when one looks beyond the pressures and tasks of the present to the necessities of shaping the life of our people in the future. The border policy of our bourgeois-patriotic-nationalistic circles is therefore particularly nonsensical because it indeed demands the greatest sacrifice of blood but holds the smallest prospects for the future of our people within itself.

Today, the German people are even less capable of sustaining themselves on their own soil than they were in peacetime. All attempts, whether through increasing land productivity itself or by cultivating the last desolate areas to increase German food production, fail to provide sustenance for our people from the resources of our own land. In fact, even the current population living in Germany would not be satisfied with the yields of our land.

Any further increase in these yields would not benefit an increase in our population but would be entirely consumed by the rise in the general living needs of individuals. Here, a standard of living is primarily established as a model through knowledge of the conditions and life in the American Union. Just as the living needs of rural areas increase through gradual awareness and the influence of city life, so too do the living needs of entire nations increase under the influence of the life of better-off, richer nations. Often, a standard of living is perceived as inadequate by a people, which only 30 years earlier would have been considered the maximum, simply because knowledge has been gained in the meantime of the standard of living of another people.

Similarly, even the lowest classes of society today consider institutions as self-evident that were considered unheard-of luxury for the upper classes 80 years ago. However, as modern technology and particularly transportation bridge distances and bring peoples closer together, their mutual relationships become more intense, and their living conditions tend to influence and attempt to align with each other. The notion that a people of a certain cultural capacity and actual cultural significance can be kept on a long-term basis through an appeal to knowledge or ideals under an otherwise universally valid standard of living is false.

Particularly, the broad masses rarely show understanding for this. They feel the need, either blaming those they believe to be responsible for it, something that is at least dangerous in democratic states, as they represent the reservoir for all revolutionary attempts, or they try to bring about a correction through their own measures, commensurate with the extent of their own knowledge and arising from their own insight. The battle against the child begins.

People want to live like others do and cannot. What could be more natural than blaming the abundance of children for this, finally having not only no joy in them anymore but trying to limit them as a burdensome evil as much as possible. Therefore, it is wrong to believe that the German people in the future could have the possibility of further reproduction through an increase in its internal land production. In the best-case scenario, the result is simply a satisfaction of increased living needs.

However, since the increase in these living needs depends on the standard of living of other peoples, who are in a much more favorable ratio of population to land, they will always lead in the provision of their lives in the future. Thus, this drive will never extinguish, and one day, either a gap will emerge between the standard of living of these peoples and those poorly supplied with land, or the latter will be forced, or at least believe they are forced, to even reduce their numbers further. The prospects for the German people are bleak.

Neither the current living space nor that achieved through a restoration of the borders of 1914 allow us to lead a life analogous to the American people. If one wanted this, then either the land of our people must be significantly expanded, or the German economy will have to return to paths known to us from the pre-war period. In both cases, power is necessary. Initially, in the sense of restoring the inner strength of our people and then, in a military sense, in the embodiment of this strength.

The national Germany of today, which sees the fulfillment of the national task in its limited border policy, cannot deceive itself that the nation's food problem will be solved in any way by this. Because even the highest success of this policy of restoring the borders of 1914 would only bring back the economic situation of 1914. In other words, the completely unresolved food question of our people would imperiously push us back into the paths of world trade, of world exports, just like today. In fact, even the German bourgeoisie and the so-called national associations with it think only in terms of economics. Production, export, and import are the catchwords juggled with, from which the salvation of the nation is hoped for in the future.

They hope that by increasing production, they can raise export capability and thereby meet the needs of imports. However, they completely forget that this whole problem for Germany, as already emphasized, is not a problem of increasing production, but a question of sales opportunities, and that the difficulty of exports would by no means be solved by lowering German production costs, as our bourgeois wiseacres suppose again. For as much as this is only partially possible in itself due to our limited domestic market, making German exports competitive by lowering production costs, for example, due to a reduction in our social legislation and the resulting obligations and burdens, would only bring us back to where we were on August 4, 1914. It really takes incredible bourgeois-national naivety to believe that England would tolerate or even could tolerate German competition that is dangerous to it.

These are the same people who know very well and always emphasize that Germany did not want the war in 1914, but was literally thrust into it. And that it was England that collected the other enmities in Europe out of pure envy of competition and unleashed them against Germany. But today, these incorrigible economic fantasists imagine that, after England risked the existence of its world empire in a tremendous world war of 4 1/2 years and remained victorious, now German competition could be viewed with different eyes than before. As if this whole question were a sporting matter for England at all.

No. England tried for decades before the war to break the threatening German economic competition, the growing German maritime trade, etc., with economic countermeasures. Only when it had to admit that this would not succeed, and on the contrary, Germany, by forming its navy, showed that it was determined to carry out its economic war truly to the peaceful conquest of the world, did England, as a last resort, invoke violence. And now, after remaining victorious, they believe the game could be repeated anew, even though Germany today is not capable at all, thanks to its domestic and foreign policies, of bringing any significant power element into play.

The attempt to restore the nutrition of our people by increasing our production and by making it cheaper will ultimately fail because, lacking a sword, one cannot take on the final consequence of this struggle. Thus, the end will be a collapse of the German people's nutrition and with it all these hopes. Apart from that, to all European states fighting as export nations for the world market, now the American Union also enters as the sharpest competitor in many areas. The size and wealth of its domestic market permit production figures and thus production facilities that so greatly reduce the product's cost that, despite the enormous wages, undercutting prices seems impossible. The development of the automotive industry may serve as a warning example here.

Not only are we Germans, for example, despite our ridiculous wages, not able to export against American competition even somewhat successfully, but we have to watch as the American car spreads in an alarming way even in our own country. This is possible because the size of its own internal sales market, the wealth of it in purchasing power and also again in raw materials, guarantees the American automotive industry internal sales figures that alone enable manufacturing methods that in Europe would simply be impossible due to the absence of these internal sales opportunities. The consequence of this is the enormous export capability of the American automotive industry. Here it is a matter of the general motorization of the world, thus a matter of an importance for the future that cannot be measured. For the American Union, the automotive industry is now at the forefront of all industries, period.

Thus, on numerous other fronts, our continent as an economic factor will increasingly come into play in an aggressive manner, thereby contributing to intensifying the struggle for the market. Considering all factors, particularly the limitation of our own raw material resources and the threatening dependence on other countries, the future of Germany must appear very bleak and sad.

But even if Germany were to overcome all economic difficulties, it would still only be where it stood on August 1914. The ultimate decision on the outcome of the struggle for the world market will lie with violence and not with the economy itself.

Our curse has been that even in peacetime, a large part of the national bourgeoisie was permeated with the belief that it could renounce violence through economic policy. And even today, its main representatives are to be found in those more or less pacifistic circles who would like to see the economy as a state-preserving, indeed even state-building force, as opponents and enemies of all heroic, ethnic virtues. However, the more a nation professes to believe that it can sustain its life solely through peaceful economic activity, the more vulnerable its economy becomes. Because ultimately, the economy is a purely secondary matter in the life of nations, bound to the primary existence of a powerful state. Before the plow, the sword must stand, and before the economy, an army.

By believing that it can do without this in Germany, the nutrition of our people must fail.

However, once a nation saturates its life with the thought that it can find its daily sustenance solely through peaceful economic activity, it will be even less likely to consider a violent solution in the event of the failure of this attempt. On the contrary, it will then try even more to take the easiest path that remedies the failure of the economy without risking bloodshed.

In fact, Germany is already in the midst of this state today. Emigration and birth control are the medicines advocated by the proponents of pacifistic economic policy and Marxist state ideology to save our nation's body.

The result of adhering to these recommendations will be particularly disastrous for Germany. Germany is racially composed of such disparate basic elements that permanent emigration inevitably draws out the more resilient, bolder, and more determined individuals from our nation. These will primarily be, as with the Vikings of old, today's carriers of Nordic blood. This slow de-Nordification of our people leads to a lowering of our overall racial value and thus to a weakening of our technical, cultural, and even state-political productive forces.

The consequences of this weakening will be particularly severe for the future because a state now enters world history as an actively acting one, which as a truly European colony has preserved the best Nordic forces of Europe for centuries through emigration, which have now, relieved by the commonality of their original blood, formed into a new national community of the highest racial value. The American Union is not coincidentally the state where by far the most, partly incredible, bold inventions are currently made. Compared to the old Europe, which has lost infinitely much of its best blood through wars and emigration, Americanism confronts it as a young, racially selected people.

Just as little as the achievement of 1000 degenerate Levantines in Europe, let's say on Crete, can be equated with the performance of 1000 racially much more valuable Germans or Englishmen, just as little can the performance of 1000 racially questionable Europeans be equated with the capacity of 1000 racially high-quality Americans. Only a consciously ethnic racial policy could save the European nations from losing the law of action to America due to the lesser value of the European peoples compared to the American one. But if the German people, instead of this, in addition to a systematic mongrelization operated by the Jew with inferior human material and a resulting lowering of its racial level per se, also lets the best carriers of blood be taken away through a continuation of emigration in hundreds and hundreds of thousands of individual cases, it will slowly sink to a people as inferior as it is incapable and worthless.

The danger is particularly great, since in complete indifference on our part, the American Union itself, stimulated by the teachings of its own racial researchers, has set special standards for immigration. By making the entry onto American soil dependent on specific racial prerequisites on the one hand and on a certain physical health of the individual per se, the bleeding of Europe from its best people has been legally and inevitably regulated. Something that our entire so-called national bourgeois world and all our economic policymakers either do not see at all or at least do not want to hear about, because it is uncomfortable for them, and because it is much cheaper to glide over these things with a few general national phrases.

To this naturally necessary reduction in the overall value of our people through emigration enforced by our economic policy, there is then the additional harm of birth control as a second damage. I have already outlined the consequences of the struggle against the child. They lie in a reduction in the number of individual beings presented to life, so that further selection can no longer take place. People then strive, on the contrary, to preserve everything that is born at all costs. However, since capability, initiative, etc., need not be associated with the first birth, but only become visible in the course of individual life's struggle, this takes away from them any possibility of sieving and selection according to such criteria.

Peoples become poor in talents and energies. Again, this is particularly bad for nations where the heterogeneity of the racial basic elements extends into the families. For according to Mendelian laws of segregation, a division of children occurs in each family into those assigned to one racial side and those to the other. But if these racial values are different in their significance for a nation, then even the value of the children of a family will be unequal for racial reasons.

It is in the interest of a people that, since by no means the first births need to reject the racially more valuable side of the two parents, life later selects at least the racially more valuable ones from the total number of children through the struggle for life, maintains the nation, and conversely puts the nation in possession of the achievements of these racially more valuable individuals. However, if man himself prevents the procreation of a larger number of children and restricts himself to first and at most second births, if these do not have the racially more valuable characteristics, he will nevertheless strive to preserve these racially inferior elements for the nation all the more. He artificially intervenes in the selection process of nature, prevents it, and thereby helps to impoverish a people of powerful personalities. He destroys the peak values of a people.

The German people, which inherently does not have the same average value as, for example, the English, but is particularly dependent on personality values. The extraordinary extremes that we can observe in the life of our people everywhere are only the secondary phenomena of our blood-mixed tornness into higher- and lower-value racial individual elements. The Englishman will generally have a better average. He may never reach the harmful depths of our people, but also never the shining heights. His life will therefore move on a more middle line and be filled with greater steadiness.

German life, on the other hand, is infinitely fluctuating and restless in everything and only gains its significance through the extraordinary achievements by which we counterbalance the questionable aspects of our national body. However, as these highest achievements are artificially deprived of their personal carriers, they themselves disappear. Our people then face a permanent impoverishment of personality values and thus a lowering of its entire cultural and intellectual significance.

If this condition persists for several hundred years, at least our German people in its general significance will be so weakened that it will no longer be entitled to be called a world people, in any case, it will no longer be able to keep pace with the achievements of the much younger, healthier American people. We will then experience with us, for a large number of reasons, what not a few ancient cultures have proven in their historical development. The Nordic blood carrier, as the most valuable racial element of culture bearers and state founders, has slowly been eliminated due to their vices and their thoughtlessness, leaving behind a mix of people of such little inner significance that the laws of action have been wrested from them to pass on to other younger and healthier peoples.

The entire southeastern Europe, especially the even older cultures of Asia Minor and Persia, as well as those of the Mesopotamian plain, provide textbook examples of the course of this process. Just as here the history was slowly shaped by the racially more valuable peoples of the Occident, so arises the danger that the significance of racially inferior Europe will slowly lead to a new determination of world destinies by the people of the North American continent. That this danger threatens all of Europe is already recognized by some today. But what it means for Germany, few want to know.

If our people continue to live into the future with the same political thoughtlessness as before, they will have to definitively abandon the claim to world importance. It will degenerate racially more and more until it finally sinks to degenerated, animalistic gluttons who will even lack the memory of past greatness. At most, within the framework of the coming world order, it will be what Switzerland and Holland were in the previous Europe. That will be the end of the life of a people whose history has been the world history for 2000 years.

With national-bourgeois foolish phrases, whose practical absurdity and worthlessness should already be proven by the successes of past developments, this fate will not be changed. Only a new reform movement, which opposes racial thoughtlessness with conscious recognition and draws all conclusions from this recognition, can still rescue our people from this abyss. It will be the task of the National Socialist movement to translate the already existing or becoming insights and scientific insights of racial doctrine and the world history clarified by it into practical applied politics.

Since the fate of Germany economically today partly also represents the fate of other nations in Europe towards America, a movement of faithful followers is again found particularly among our people who wish to counterpose Europe to the Union of American States in order to prevent an impending world hegemony of the North American continent.

The pan-European movement seems to have something at least initially appealing to it. Yes, if world history could be judged by economic criteria, that might even be true. For the historian and thus mechanical politician, two are always more than one. But in the life of nations, it is not numbers that decide, but values.

That the American Union is able to rise to such a threatening height is not based on the fact that there . . . millions of people form a state, but on the fact that . . . millions of square kilometers of the most fertile and richest soil are inhabited by . . . millions of people of the highest racial value.

[Whereas the fact that] That these people, despite the spatial magnitude of their habitat, form a state, has an increased significance for the other world, inasmuch as a summarizing organization exists, thanks to which the racially conditioned individual worth of these people can find a closed overall application for fighting the struggle of life.

If this were not correct, if the significance of the American Union were only in the number of people alone or also in the size of the space or in the ratio in which this space stands to the number of people, then for Europe

Russia would be at least equally dangerous. Today's Russia encompasses . . . millions of people over . . . million square kilometers. These people are also organized in a state entity, whose value, traditionally taken, should even be higher than that of the American Union, yet it will never occur to anyone to fear Russian hegemony for the world because of that. The number of the Russian people does not have such an inner value that this number could become a danger to the freedom of the world. At least not in terms of economic and power-political domination of the other earth, but at most in that of a flood with disease bacilli, which currently have their focus in Russia.

However, if the significance of the impending American hegemony position appears to be primarily determined by the value of the American people and only secondarily by the size of the living space given to this people and the thereby favorable ratio between population and land area, then this hegemony will not be eliminated by a purely formal numerical merger of European peoples, unless their inner value is higher than that of the American Union. Otherwise, this American Union should particularly regard present-day Russia as the highest danger, as even more so the China populated with over 400 million people.

Thus, the pan-European movement is fundamentally based on the fundamental misconception that human values could be replaced by human numbers. This is a purely mechanical view of history that shies away from exploring all the formative forces of life, instead seeing both the creative sources of human culture and the factors shaping history in numerical majorities. This view corresponds to the senselessness of our Western democracy as much as to the cowardly pacifism of our over-economic circles. That it is the ideal of all inferior or semi-racial bastards is obvious. Likewise, the Jew particularly welcomes such a view, as its consistent pursuit leads to racial chaos and confusion, to bastardization and negrification of cultured humanity, and ultimately to such a lowering of its racial value that the Hebrew who keeps himself apart may slowly rise to become the ruler of the world. At least he imagines he might one day rise to the rank of the brain of this devalued humanity.

However, aside from this fundamental misconception of the pan-European movement, the idea of a merger of European peoples under the compulsion of a general awareness of impending distress is a fantastic, historically impossible folly. I do not mean to say that such a merger under Jewish protection and on Jewish initiative would be impossible in itself, but only that the result could not correspond to the hopes, around which the whole enchantment is staged. For one should not believe that such a European coalition could mobilize any force that would appear outwardly. It is an old experience that lasting alliances of peoples can only take place when racially equivalent and related peoples are involved and when, secondly, their merger takes place in the form of the slow process of a hegemonic struggle.

Thus, Rome once subjugated the Latin states one by one until finally its strength sufficed to become the focal point of a world empire. But this is also the history of the emergence of the British Empire. Thus, Prussia ended the German state disunity, and thus, entirely alone in this way, a Europe could once emerge that represents the interests of its population in a unified state form. However, this could only be the result of centuries of struggle, as an infinite number of old traditions and customs would have to be overcome, and an approximation of peoples would have to take place, which already racially diverge extraordinarily. The difficulty of giving such an entity a unified state language could also only be resolved in a process lasting centuries.

All of this, however, would not be the fulfillment realization of today's pan-European ideas, but the success of the struggle for existence of the most powerful nation in Europe, and what would remain then would be as little a Pan-Europe as the unification of the Latin states once was a Pan-Latin. The power that once carried out this process of unification in centuries-long struggles has forever given the entire structure its name. And the power that would now naturally create a Pan-Europe would at the same time also rob it of the designation Pan-Europe.

But even in this case, the desired success would be lacking. For just as today any European great power - and it could only be one valuable to its people, thus racially significant power - were to bring Europe together in this way, the final completion of this unity would mean the racial lowering of its founders and thus ultimately deprive the entire structure of its ultimate value. One could never create a structure that could stand up to the American Union.

In the future, North America will only be able to confront the state that has managed to raise the value of its people racially through the nature of its inner life as well as through the sense of its external politics and to bring it into the most suitable form for this purpose. However, by presenting such a solution as possible, a whole number of nations will be able to participate in it, which can and will lead to increased capability due to mutual competition.

It is once again the task of the National Socialist movement to strengthen and prepare its own homeland to the utmost for this task.

However, attempting to realize the pan-European idea through a purely formal merger of European peoples, without being forced by a European hegemon in centuries-long struggles, would lead to a structure whose entire strength and energy would be absorbed by internal rivalries and disputes, just as the strength of the German tribes was once absorbed in the German Confederation. Only when the internal German question was finally resolved by the superiority of Prussia could a united national effort be made outwardly. However, it is reckless to believe that the confrontation between Europe and America would always be of an economic and peaceful nature when economic factors finally become decisive factors in life. It was inherent in the nature of the formation of the North American state that it initially showed little interest in foreign policy issues. Not only due to the lack of a long state tradition, but simply due to the fact that the natural expansionist drive of people within the American continent itself had extremely wide areas available.

Therefore, the policy of the American Union from the moment of its separation from the European mother states until the present time was primarily domestic policy. Indeed, the struggles for freedom themselves were essentially nothing more than the shedding of external political ties in favor of a life thought of exclusively in terms of domestic politics. However, to the extent that the American people have increasingly fulfilled the tasks of internal colonization, the natural activist drive, which is particularly characteristic of young nations, will turn outward. But the surprises that the world may still experience would be least resisted by a pacifist-democratic-pan-European state of confusion. According to the common bastardized conception of Coudenhove, this Paneuropa would eventually play the same role against the American Union or a nationally awakened China as the old Austrian state did against Germany or Russia.

Truly, the opinion that because a merging of people of various ethnic backgrounds has occurred in the American Union, this should also be possible in Europe, does not need to be refuted. However, upon closer examination, it becomes clear that the overwhelming majority of these various ethnic groups belong to racially similar or at least related basic elements. This is because the emigration process in Europe was a process of selection of the most capable, and this capability, in all European peoples, primarily lay in the Nordic elements. Thus, the American Union actually extracted the scattered Nordic elements from inherently very different peoples.

It should also be considered that already in the last century this process of merging became increasingly difficult, as Europeans went to North America under the pressure of necessity, who, as members of European nation-states, not only felt culturally connected to them but also valued their national traditions more highly than citizenship in their new homeland. Moreover, the American Union also failed to assimilate people of entirely different races with strongly developed national feelings or racial instincts. The assimilation power of the American Union failed with regard to both the Chinese and Japanese elements. One feels this precisely and knows it, and therefore would prefer to exclude these foreigners from immigration. However, the American immigration policy itself confirms that the previous merging indeed required people of certain uniform racial foundations and immediately fails when dealing with fundamentally different people.

The fact that the American Union itself feels like a Nordic-Germanic state and not as an international mix of peoples is also evident from the way immigration quotas are allocated to European peoples. Scandinavians, including Swedes, Norwegians, followed by Danes, then English, and finally Germans, are allocated the largest quotas. Romance and Slavic peoples receive very small quotas, while Japanese and Chinese would preferably be excluded altogether. Wanting to oppose a European coalition or a Paneurope, consisting of Mongols, Slavs, Germans, Romance peoples, etc., in which anything but Germanic peoples would dominate, to this predominantly Nordic state, is a utopia.

However, it is a very dangerous utopia, considering that many countless Germans see a rosy future without having to make the most severe sacrifices for it. The fact that this utopia is emerging precisely from Austria is not without a certain irony. After all, this state and its fate are the liveliest examples of the enormous power inherent in such artificially pieced together, but inherently unnatural formations. It is the rootless spirit of the old imperial capital Vienna, that hybrid city of East and West, which speaks to us in this regard.

19

CHAPTER 10
No Neutrality

28

In summary, it can be said once again that our bourgeois-national politics, whose foreign policy goal is the restoration of the borders of the year 1914, is nonsensical, indeed disastrous. It inevitably brings us into conflict with all states that participated in the World War. It thereby guarantees the further existence of the coalition of victors that slowly strangles us.

It ensures France a favorable public opinion in the rest of the world for its eternal action against Germany. Even if it were successful, it would mean nothing for the German future in the end but still force us to fight with blood and steel. Furthermore, it prevents any stability in German foreign policy altogether.

A characteristic of our pre-war politics was that it had to give the impression to outside observers of decisions that were as wavering as they were often inscrutable. Aside from the Triple Alliance itself, the preservation of which could not have been a foreign policy end but only a means to such an end, one cannot discern a stable idea guiding the fate of our people in the pre-war period. This is naturally incomprehensible.

The moment the foreign policy goal was no longer to fight for the interests of the German people but to maintain world peace, we lost ground beneath our feet. I can clearly outline a people's interests, define them, and keep the great goal in mind regardless of the individual possibilities of representing them. Gradually, the rest of humanity will also gain general knowledge of a people's specific leading foreign policy thoughts. This then allows for a more lasting regulation of relations among themselves, be it in the sense of intended resistance against the recognized actions of such a power or a simple acknowledgment of it, or even in the sense of an understanding, as own interests might be achieved through mutual means.

This stability in foreign policy can be observed in a number of European states. Russia has shown certain foreign policy goals during long periods of its development, which then govern its entire actions. France has represented consistently even-handed foreign policy intentions over centuries, regardless of who embodied political power in Paris at any given time. One should not only speak of England as a state of traditional diplomacy, but above all as a state of foreign policy idea that has become tradition. With Germany, such an idea was only periodically discernible in the Prussian state.

In the short time of Bismarckian statesmanship, we see Prussia fulfilling its German mission, but with that, every far-reaching foreign policy goal also ends. The new German Reich has not possessed such a goal, especially since Bismarck's departure, as the slogan of maintaining peace, and thus maintaining a given state, possesses no stable content or character. Just as any passive slogan is in reality condemned to be a plaything of offensive will. Only those who want to act can determine their actions according to their will.

Therefore, the Triple Entente, which wanted to act, had all the advantages inherent in the self-determination of action, while the Triple Alliance, with its more contemplative tendency to maintain world peace, was at a disadvantage to the same degree. Thus, the war was also determined in timing and initiation by the nations with specific foreign policy goals, while conversely, the Triple Alliance powers were surprised by it at a time that could hardly have been less favorable. If Germany had even the slightest intention of war, then it would have been possible, through a number of measures that could have been carried out effortlessly, to give the beginning of the war a completely different appearance. But Germany had no specific foreign policy goal in mind, did not think of any aggressive steps to achieve this goal, and as a result, was surprised by the events.

From Austria-Hungary, one could not hope for any other foreign policy goal than to wind its way through the vicissitudes of European politics, so that the decrepit state entity did not clash anywhere, thereby being able to hide the true inner character of this monstrous state corpse from the world.

The German national bourgeoisie, of which I can only speak here, as international Marxism inherently only knows the goal of Germany's destruction, has not learned anything from the past even today. Even today, one does not feel the necessity to set a foreign policy goal for the nation that may be considered satisfactory for the German future, thereby giving our foreign policy endeavors a certain stability for a more or less extended period. Because only when such a possible foreign policy goal appears fundamentally delineated can one discuss the possibilities that may lead to success in detail.

Only then does politics enter the stage of the art of the possible. As long as this entire political life is not governed by any guiding thought, individual actions will not have the character of utilizing all possibilities to achieve a specific success in themselves, but they will always be individual stations on the path of aimless meandering from today to tomorrow. Then, above all, that persistence required for the prosecution of great goals will be lost, meaning: today one will try this and tomorrow that, the day after tomorrow one will consider this foreign policy possibility and suddenly embrace a completely wrong intention, unless this apparent chaos ultimately corresponds to the wishes of that power that governs Germany today and truly does not want our people to ever rise again.

Only international Jewry can possess a living interest in a German foreign policy that, through its eternally unreasonable leaps, lacks that clear plan, and whose only justification is: Yes, of course, we also don't know what should be done, but we do something because something must be done. Indeed, one can often hear precisely these people being so little convinced of the inner meaning of their foreign policy actions that their highest motivation can only be to ask whether someone else knows something better. That is the foundation on which the statecraft of a Gustav Stresemann rests.

In contrast, it is more necessary today than ever that the German people set themselves a foreign policy goal that meets their real internal needs and, conversely, grants their foreign policy actions for the foreseeable future an unconditional stability. Because only if our people fundamentally determine their interests in this way and then steadfastly defend them can they hope to persuade one or another state, whose interests are now definitively aligned with ours, or even concurrent, to enter into closer ties with Germany. Because the idea of solving our people's plight from the League of Nations is just as unjustified as it was to let the German question be decided by the Frankfurt Federal Parliament.

In the League of Nations, the saturated nations dominate. Yes, it is their instrument. They largely have no interest in allowing a change in the distribution of the earth's space, as it would again speak in their favor. And when they talk about the rights of small nations, they are actually only concerned with the interests of the largest.

If Germany is to achieve true freedom once again, in order to provide the German people with daily bread under its blessing, then it will have to take measures for this outside the League of Nations parliament in Geneva. But then it will be necessary for it to find allies, lacking sufficient strength, who can believe that by aligning with Germany, they can also serve their own interests. However, such a condition will never arise unless these nations fully understand Germany's real foreign policy goal.

And above all, Germany itself will never maintain the strength and inner fortitude necessary to overcome the resistances of world history if the real foreign policy goal is not completely clear to these nations. It will never learn to be patient in detail and, if necessary, to make sacrifices in order to finally achieve the vital goal on a large scale. For even among allies, relations will never be entirely smooth.

Disturbances in mutual relations will always arise, potentially taking on threatening forms, if the strength to overcome minor inconveniences and resistances is not found in the magnitude of the foreign policy goal once set. Here, the French leadership in the decades before the war can serve as an exemplary model. Unlike our perpetually whining, often barking at the moon hoorah-patriots, it overlooked everything small, even remaining silent in the face of very bitter incidents, in order not to lose the possibility of organizing a revenge war against Germany.

The setting of a clear foreign policy goal is particularly important because otherwise, representatives of other interests within one's own nation will always be able to confuse public opinion and use small, sometimes even provoked incidents as a pretext to change the foreign policy opinion. Thus, France will always try to create dissension and even alienation among peoples from small quarrels, either arising from the situation itself or artificially fabricated, despite their dependence on each other based on the nature of their real life interests and the need for joint action against France. Such attempts will always succeed if, due to the absence of an immutable foreign policy goal, one's own political actions lack true stability and, above all, if there is a lack of perseverance in preparing measures conducive to fulfilling one's own political objectives.

The German people, who possess neither a foreign policy tradition nor a foreign policy goal, will always be inclined to indulge in utopian ideals and neglect their real life interests. For what has our people not romanticized over the past 100 years? Soon it was Greeks whom we wanted to save from the Turks, then Turks to whom we showed our affection against Russians and Italians, then our people found enchantment in supporting Polish freedom fighters, only to sympathize with Boers, and so on and so forth. But what have all these foolish outpourings of a politically inept and talkative soul cost our people?

Thus, the relationship with Austria, as it was proudly emphasized, was not one of sober reason, but a true inner bond of hearts. If only reason had spoken instead of the heart back then, and if reason had decided, then Germany would be saved today. However, precisely because we are a people that allows its political actions to be determined too little by reasons of real rational understanding, and because we cannot look back on any great political tradition, we must at least give our people an immutable foreign policy goal for the future that appears suitable to make political measures of state leadership understandable to the broad masses.

Only in this way will it be possible for millions to stand behind a state leadership in a foreboding belief that implements decisions that may have some painful aspects. This is a prerequisite for bringing about mutual understanding between the people and the state leadership, and indeed also a prerequisite for anchoring a certain tradition in the state leadership itself. It is not acceptable for every German government to have its own foreign policy goal. One can argue about the means, dispute them, but the goal itself must be fixed once and for all as unchangeable. Then politics can become the great art of the possible, meaning that it remains reserved for the genius abilities of individual statesmen to perceive the possibilities that bring the people and the Reich closer to their foreign policy goal from case to case.

This foreign policy goal setting is completely absent in present-day Germany. Therefore, the boundless, fluctuating, and uncertain manner of perceiving the interests of our people is also understandable, as is the entire confusion of our public opinion, and also those incredible zigzags of our foreign policy, which always end unhappily without the people being capable of judging the responsible parties to truly hold them accountable. No, they don't know what to do.

Yes, there are indeed quite a few people today who believe that one must not do anything at all. They summarize their opinion to the effect that Germany must be clever and restrained today, that it must not engage anywhere, that it must keep an eye on the development of events, but refrain from participating itself, in order to one day assume the role of that laughing third party who reaps success while two others argue.

Yes, yes, that's how clever and wise our present-day bourgeois statesmen are. A political judgment untainted by any knowledge of history. There are not a few proverbs that have become a real curse for our people. For example, "The smarter one gives in" or "Clothes make the man" or "With the hat in hand, one can travel through the whole country" or even "When two quarrel, the third rejoices."

In the life of nations at least, this last proverb only applies to a limited extent, [And this for the following reason], namely, when two within a nation quarrel hopelessly, then a third party outside the nation can win. In the life of nations among each other, however, states will always have the final success for themselves that consciously fight, because only in conflict lies the possibility of increasing their strength. There is no historical event in the world that could not be judged from two perspectives. The neutrals always face the interventionists on one side. And generally, the neutrals will come up short, while the interventionists can claim success more readily, provided that the party they support does not lose.

In the life of nations, this means the following: When two powerful entities on this earth quarrel, the surrounding smaller or larger states may participate in this struggle to a greater or lesser extent or stay away from it. In one case, the possibility of gain is not excluded if participation occurs on the side that achieves victory. However, regardless of who wins, the neutrals will never have another fate than enmity with the remaining victorious state.

None of the great powers on earth has risen through neutrality as a principle of political action, but only through struggle. If there are dominant power states on earth, smaller nations have no choice but to either give up on their future altogether or to fight under the protection of favorable coalitions and thereby increase their own strength. Because the role of the laughing third party always presupposes that this third party already has power. However, one who is always neutral will never become a power.

For as much as a nation's power lies in its inner value, it finds its ultimate expression in the organizational form of a nation's combat forces on the battlefield, created by the will of this inner value. However, this form will never arise if it is not subjected to practical testing from time to time. The eternal values of a nation are forged into steel and iron under the hammer of world history. But those who avoid battles will never gain the strength to fight battles. And those who never fight battles will never be the heirs of those who struggle in sword combat. For the heirs of world history so far have not been nations with cowardly notions of neutrality, but rather young nations of the better sword. Neither antiquity, nor the Middle Ages, nor modern times know of any example of powerful states emerging in any other way than through constant struggle.

The historical heirs, however, have always been states of power. Certainly, in the life of nations, a third party can be the heir when two quarrel, but then this third party is already from the outset the power that consciously lets two others quarrel in order to definitively crush them without great sacrifices of its own. Thus, neutrality loses the character of passive participation in events altogether and instead assumes that of a conscious political operation. Naturally, no wise state leadership will start a fight without weighing the magnitude of its potential own commitment and comparing it with the magnitude of the opponent's. However, if it recognizes the impossibility of being able to fight against a certain power, then it will be all the more compelled to try to fight alongside that power. For from this joint struggle, the formerly weaker party can gain the strength to defend its own vital interests even against this power if necessary.

Let it not be said that no power will enter into an alliance with a state that may one day itself become a threat. Alliances do not represent political purposes, but only means to those purposes. We must use them today, even if we know a thousand times that later developments may lead to the opposite. There is no alliance with eternal duration. Blessed are the nations that, due to the complete divergence of their interests, are able to enter into a federal relationship for a certain time without being forced into mutual conflict upon its termination. However, especially a weak state that aspires to power and greatness will always have to try to actively participate in the general political events of world history.

When Prussia entered its Silesian War, this was also a relatively minor event compared to the huge confrontation between England and France, which was already in full swing at the time. Perhaps one could accuse Frederick the Great of having fetched English chestnuts from the fire. But would Prussia ever have arisen, with which a Bismarck could create a new German Empire, if at that time a prince had sat on the throne of Hohenzollern who, in recognition of the upcoming greater events of world history, had kept his Prussia in pious neutrality?

The three Silesian Wars brought Prussia more than Silesia. On these battlefields, those regiments grew up that in the subsequent period carried the German flags from Weißenburg and Wörth to Sedan, to finally greet the new emperor of the new empire in the Hall of Mirrors of the Versailles Palace. Indeed, at that time Prussia was a small state, insignificant in terms of population and territorial size, but by leaping into the great actions of world history, this small state acquired the legitimacy for the foundation of the later German Empire.

And once, in this Prussian state, the neutralists also prevailed. That was during the period of Napoleon I. At that time, it was initially believed that Prussia could be kept neutral, and later it was punished with the most terrible defeat for it. Even in the year 1812, the two views stood sharply opposed. Some advocated neutrality, while others, led by Baron von Stein, advocated intervention. The fact that the neutralists prevailed in 1812 cost Prussia and Germany infinite blood and infinite suffering. And the fact that finally, in 1813, the interventionists prevailed, saved Prussia.

The clearest answer to the opinion that political success could be achieved by maintaining cautious neutrality as a third power was given by the World War. What did the neutrals of the World War practically achieve? Were they the laughing third parties? Or does one believe that Germany would play a different role in a similar event? It should not be assumed that only the magnitude of the World War was to blame.

No, in the future, all wars involving major nations will be gigantic national wars. However, in any European confrontation in the future, Germany as a neutral state would have no greater significance than Holland or Switzerland or Denmark, etc., in the World War. Does one really believe that, after the events, we would have the strength to play the role against a remaining victor that we did not dare to play in alliance with one of the two combatants?

The World War has indisputably proven one thing: Whoever remains neutral in major world historical conflicts may initially be able to conduct small transactions, but from a power-political perspective, they will definitely withdraw from any participation in the destinies of the world.

If the American Union had maintained its neutrality in the World War, regardless of whether England or Germany emerged as the victor, the American Union would be regarded today as a second-rate power. Its entry into the war lifted it maritally to the strength of England but politically to a power of decisive importance. The assessment of the American Union since its entry into the World War has completely changed. It is in the nature of humanity's forgetfulness not to remember, after a short time, what general assessment a state of affairs had found a few years earlier. Just as we can now discern from the speeches of many foreign statesmen the complete disregard for Germany's former greatness, we are similarly unable to estimate the extent of the increase in value that the American Union has experienced in our own judgment since entering the World War.

This is also the most statesmanlike justification for Italy's entry into the war against its former ally. If Italy had not taken this step, it would today share the role of Spain, regardless of how the dice had fallen. The fact that it took the much-maligned step of actively participating in the World War brought it an increase in its position and a strengthening of it, which has found its final crowning expression in fascism. Without entry into the war, fascism would also have been a completely unthinkable phenomenon.

The German can think bitterly or not bitterly about this. It is important to learn from history, especially when its lessons speak to us in such a compelling manner.

Thus, the belief that by maintaining cautious and restrained neutrality towards the developing conflicts in Europe and elsewhere, one day reaping the rewards as a laughing third party, is false and foolish. Freedom is not obtained through begging or cheating, nor through work and diligence, but exclusively through struggle, and indeed, through one's own struggle. It is very possible that willpower is valued more than action.

Often, nations have achieved success within the framework of prudent alliance policies that did not correspond to the magnitude of their military achievements. Fate does not always measure a nation that boldly commits itself based on the extent of its deeds, but very often based on the magnitude of its will. The history of the Italian unification of the 19th century is remarkable in this regard. Similarly, the World War demonstrates how a whole host of states achieved extraordinary political success less through their military achievements than through the audacious boldness with which they took sides and the perseverance with which they persevered.

Under all circumstances, if Germany is to end its period of enslavement by all, it must attempt to actively penetrate into a combination of powers in order to participate actively in the power-political future shaping of European life. The objection that such participation carries a heavy risk is correct. But does one truly believe that freedom can be obtained without taking risks? Or does one think that there has ever been an act in world history that was not associated with risk? Was the decision of Frederick the Great to enter the first Silesian War without risk? Or was the unification of Germany by Bismarck risk-free? No, and a thousand times no! Everything from the birth of man to his death is questionable. What appears certain is only death alone. That is why the final stake is not the hardest, as it will be demanded one day one way or another.

Of course, it is a question of statesmanship to choose the stake in such a way that the highest possible gain is obtained. But to refrain from betting altogether out of fear of possibly picking the wrong horse means relinquishing the future of a nation. The objection that such action then has the character of a gamble can be most easily refuted by simply pointing to past historical experience.

A gamble is a game whose profit possibilities are entirely subject to the determination of chance from the outset. This will never be the case in politics. For as much as the final decision lies in the darkness of the future, so much does the conviction of the possibility or impossibility of success build upon humanly recognizable factors.

Weighing these factors is the task of the political leadership of the people. The result of this examination must then lead to a decision. Thus, this decision springs from one's own insight and is carried by the belief in the possible success based on this insight. I can therefore only call a politically decisive act a gamble only because its outcome is not 100 percent certain, as I may do with an operation performed by a doctor, whose outcome also may not necessarily be successful. It has always been the nature of great men to carry out even doubtful, uncertainly successful actions with utmost energy, if the necessity was present and after the most thorough examination of all circumstances, only this one particular action remained in question.

The willingness to make significant decisions in the struggle among nations will be all the higher, the more the acting individuals, upon considering their nation, can be convinced that even a failure will not be able to destroy the vitality of the nation. For an internally healthy nation will never be able to be extinguished by defeats on the battlefield in the long run. Therefore, if a nation possesses this internal health, assuming sufficient racial significance, the courage to undertake difficult operations can be greater, since even the failure of such operations would not necessarily mean the downfall of such a nation.

And in this regard, Clausewitz is correct when he states in his confession that for a healthy nation, such a defeat can once again lead to a later rise, but conversely, only cowardly submission, that is, passive surrender to fate, can lead to ultimate destruction. However, the neutrality that is touted today as the only possible action for our people is actually nothing more than a willful surrender to a fate determined by foreign powers. And therein lies the characteristic and possibility of our decline. If, on the other hand, our people had undertaken failed attempts at freedom themselves, there would already be a factor in the expression of this attitude that would benefit the vitality of our nation.

For one should not say that it is statesmanlike prudence that holds us back from such steps. No, it is pitiful cowardice and lack of conviction that, in this case, as so often in history, is attempted to be mistaken for prudence. Of course, a nation may, under the pressure of foreign powers, be forced to endure foreign oppression for years.

However, as little as a nation can then accomplish anything serious externally against overpowering forces, so much will its inner life strive for freedom and leave nothing untried that could change the current state one day with the use of the entire strength of such a people. One will then endure the yoke of foreign conquerors, but with clenched fists and gritted teeth, one will wait for the moment that provides the first opportunity to rid oneself of the tyrant. Such a thing may be possible under the pressure of circumstances.

But what presents itself today as statesmanlike prudence is actually a spirit of voluntary submission, of lack of conviction in resisting, indeed, shameless persecution of those who dare to think of such resistance and whose work could evidently serve the resurgence of their people. It is the spirit of internal disarmament, the destruction of all moral factors that could once serve the revival of this people and state, and this spirit truly cannot pose as statesmanlike prudence, for it is indeed state-destroying dishonor. And this spirit must indeed hate any attempt by our people to actively participate in the upcoming European development because already in the mere attempt to participate lies the necessity of the fight against this spirit.

However, if a government appears to be attacked by the rot of this spirit, then it is the task of the opposition, perceiving and representing the real life forces of a people, and thus representing them, to write the struggle for national uplift and thereby for national honor on their banners. It must not be intimidated by the assertion that foreign policy is the task of the responsible government, since such a responsible leadership no longer exists, but rather it must declare itself committed to the view that in addition to the formal rights of the respective governments, there are eternal obligations that compel every member of a people to do what is recognized as necessary for the existence of the national community. Even if this stands in stark contrast to the intentions of bad and incompetent governments.

Therefore, especially in Germany today, the so-called national opposition has the highest obligation, considering the unworthiness of the general leadership of our people, to set a clear external political goal and to prepare and educate our people for the implementation of these thoughts. It must first and foremost declare the most vigorous war against the widespread hope today that by actively participating in the League of Nations, we can change our fate. Overall, it must ensure that our people slowly recognize that we cannot expect the improvement of the German situation from institutions whose representatives are the beneficiaries of our current misfortune.

Furthermore, it must deepen the conviction that without the reclamation of German freedom, all social hopes are utopian promises without any real value. It must also bring our people to the realization that only the exertion of our own strength is in question for this freedom. Therefore, our entire domestic and foreign policy must be one under which the inner strength of our people grows and increases. And finally, it must enlighten the people that this exertion of strength must be for a truly valuable goal and that we will need allies for this purpose, as we cannot face destiny alone.

---- 19 ----

CHAPTER 11
Germany's Political Situation

---- 28 ----

For the question of the future shaping of German foreign policy, apart from the inner strength of our people, its character strength and assessment, the magnitude of its potential military engagement, as well as the relationship of these power means to those of the surrounding states, are of decisive importance.

I need not elaborate further in this work on the moral inner weakness of our people today. Our general weaknesses, partly based on blood, partly inherent in the nature of our current state organization, or attributable to the actions of our poor leadership, are perhaps better known to the rest of the world than to the German public. A large part of the measures of our oppressors is based on the recognition of these weaknesses. However, amidst all acknowledgment of the actual conditions, it must never be forgotten that the same people today, barely 10 years ago, accomplished historically unparalleled achievements.

The German people, who currently leave such a sad impression, have nevertheless repeatedly demonstrated their immense value in world history. The World War itself is the most glorious testimony to the heroic spirit and sacrifice of our people, to their death-defying discipline, and to their ingenious ability in a thousand and one areas of organizing their lives. Even its purely military leadership has achieved immortal successes. Only the political leadership had failed. It was already the precursor of what is even worse today.

So, even if the inner qualities of our people today may be unsatisfactory a thousand times over, they will present a different picture with a single stroke, once a different hand takes the reins of events to lead our people out of their current decline. How wonderful the adaptability of our people is, we see in our history. Prussia in 1806 and Prussia in 1813.

What a difference.

In 1806, the state of the saddest capitulation on all fronts, of an unheard-of wretchedness of civic sentiment, and in 1813, the state of the most fervent hatred against foreign rule and the most patriotic spirit of sacrifice for the own people, of the most heroic determination for freedom. What really changed back then? The people? No, it remained the same in its inner essence as before, only its leadership had passed into different hands. The weakness of the Prussian government in the post-Frederician period, the ossified and outdated leadership of the army, was now followed by a new spirit. Freiherr von [sic] Stein and Gneisenau, Scharnhorst, Clausewitz, and Blücher were the representatives of the new Prussia. And the world had almost forgotten in a few months that this Prussia had experienced a Jena seven years earlier.

And was it any different before the new foundation of the Reich? Barely a decade had sufficed to turn German decline, German disunity, and general political dishonor into a new empire, which seemed to many to be the most powerful embodiment of German power and glory. A single towering figure, in the struggle against the mediocrity of the majorities, gave German genius the freedom of its development again. Imagine Bismarck removed from our history, and only abject mediocrity would fill the time that has been the most glorious for our people for centuries.

Just as the German people could be plunged from its unprecedented greatness into its current chaos within a few years by the mediocrity of its leadership, so can it be lifted up again by an iron fist. Its inner worth will then become so visible to the whole world that the fact of its existence alone must compel attention and assessment.

But if this value is initially dormant, it is all the more necessary to gain clarity about Germany's current real power value.

I have already attempted to outline a brief picture of Germany's current military instrument, the Reichswehr. At this point, I want to sketch the general military situation of Germany in relation to the surrounding world.

Germany is currently surrounded by three power factors or groups.

England, Russia, and France are presently the most militarily threatening neighbors of Germany. The French power appears strengthened by a system of European alliances, which extends from Paris through Warsaw, Prague to Belgrade.

Germany is wedged between these states with completely open borders. What is particularly threatening is that the western border of the Reich runs through Germany's largest industrial area. This western border, however, also offers only limited possibilities for defense due to its length and the lack of any real natural barriers.

The attempt to consider the Rhine as a militarily effective line of defense is also futile. Not only has Germany been deprived of the opportunity to make the necessary technical preparations for this by the peace treaties, but the river itself presents few obstacles to the passage of modern equipped armies, especially as the limited means of German defense would have to be spread too thinly along such a long front. Furthermore, the Rhine runs through Germany's largest industrial area, so a struggle for it would mean the destruction of the most technologically important industrial centers and factories vital for national defense from the outset.

If, due to a German-French conflict, Czechoslovakia were to become another opponent for Germany, then a second major industrial area, Saxony, would be exposed to the highest risk of war. Here, too, the border runs naturally unprotected down to Bavaria, so extensive and open that effective resistance would hardly be feasible. If Poland were to participate in such a conflict as well, then the entire eastern border, apart from a few inadequate fortifications, would also be open to attack.

While, on the one hand, the German borders are militarily unprotected and open in long lines surrounded by adversaries, our North Sea coast is particularly small and confined. The maritime resources for its defense are laughable and essentially worthless. The naval vessels we possess today, starting from our so-called battleships, are at best target practice material for enemy shooting exercises.

The few newly built, modern light cruisers have no decisive value whatsoever. Even for the Baltic Sea, the fleet allotted to us is insufficient. All in all, the only value of our fleet is at most that of a floating shooting range.

Therefore, in the event of a conflict with any sea power, not only would German trade be immediately terminated, but the risk of landings would also be present.

The entire unfavorable aspect of our military situation arises from the following consideration: The capital of the Reich, Berlin, is just under 175 km away from the Polish border. It is approximately 190 km from the nearest Czech border, and the same distance applies as the crow flies to Wismar and the Stettiner Haff. This means that from these borders, Berlin can be reached by modern aircraft in less than 1 hour. Drawing a line 60 km east of the Rhine, almost the entire western German industrial area lies within it. From Frankfurt to Dortmund, there is hardly a major German industrial center that does not lie within this zone. As long as France occupies part of the left bank of the Rhine, it is thus able to advance into the heart of our western German industrial area with airplanes in barely 30 minutes.

The distance from Munich to the Czech border is the same as Berlin's from the Polish and Czech borders. Czech military aircraft would take about 60 minutes to reach Munich, 40 minutes to reach Nuremberg, and 30 minutes to reach Regensburg. Even Augsburg is only 200 km away from the Czech border and could therefore be easily reached in just under an hour with today's aircraft.

Almost as far as Augsburg is from the Czech border in a straight line, is its distance from the French border. From Augsburg to Strasbourg, the straight-line distance is 230 km, but to the nearest French border, it is only 210 km. This places Augsburg within a zone that could be reached by hostile aircraft within an hour. In fact, when examining the German border from this perspective, it becomes apparent that within an hour of flight time, the following areas could be reached: the entire industrial area in western Germany including Osnabrück, Bielefeld, Kassel, Würzburg, Stuttgart, and Augsburg. In the east: Munich, Augsburg, Würzburg, Magdeburg, Berlin, and Stettin. In other words, given the current state of the German borders, there is only a very small area, covering a few square kilometers, that could not be visited by hostile aircraft within the first hour.

In this context, France is considered the most dangerous adversary because, thanks to its alliances, it alone is able to threaten almost all of Germany with aircraft within an hour of the outbreak of a conflict. Germany's military countermeasures against the use of this weapon are currently negligible.

Just this single consideration shows the dismal situation in which German resistance would immediately find itself if left to its own devices against France. Those who have often been exposed to the effects of enemy air raids in the field know best how to assess the moral effects that result from them.

But even Hamburg and Bremen, indeed all our coastal cities, would not escape this fate today, since the great navies now possess the ability to bring floating landing platforms very close to the coast using aircraft carriers.

However, Germany not only lacks effective weapons in sufficient quantities to counter aircraft attacks today but also in other respects, the purely technical equipment of our small Reichswehr is hopelessly inferior to that of our adversaries. The lack of heavy artillery could be more easily tolerated than the lack of a genuinely promising defense against tank weapons. If Germany were to be thrust into war against France and its allies today, without being able to make at least the most essential preparations for defense beforehand, then the decision would be made in favor of our opponents within a few days due to their purely technical superiority. In the heat of battle, the measures necessary to defend against such a hostile attack could no longer be prepared.

The belief that improvisational means could at least offer resistance for a certain period of time is also incorrect because these improvisations would still require a certain amount of time, which, however, does not appear to be available in the event of a conflict. Events would unfold more rapidly and create facts than would leave us any time to organize countermeasures against these events.

Therefore, we can consider the foreign policy possibilities of any side, but one scenario is fundamentally excluded for Germany: we will never be able to proceed against the forces currently mobilized in Europe relying solely on our own military power. Any combination that would bring Germany into conflict with France, England, Poland, Czechoslovakia, etc., without giving it the opportunity for thorough preparation, is thus ruled out.

This fundamental realization is important because there are still well-intentioned national men in Germany today who believe in all seriousness that we must ally with Russia.

Purely from a military perspective, such a notion is unfeasible or even disastrous for Germany. Just as before the year 1914, we can today consider it an absolute certainty that in any conflict involving Germany, regardless of the reasons or circumstances, France will always be our adversary. Whatever European combinations may emerge in the future, France will always side against Germany. This is deeply ingrained in the traditional sense of French foreign policy.

It is wrong to believe that the outcome of the war has changed this fact. On the contrary, the World War did not bring about the complete fulfillment of France's war aim. This goal was by no means limited to the recovery of Alsace-Lorraine; on the contrary, Alsace-Lorraine itself represents only a small step in the direction of France's foreign policy goal. The possession of Alsace-Lorraine does not negate the aggressive tendencies of French policy towards Germany, as evidenced most clearly by the fact that even during the time when France already possessed Alsace-Lorraine, the anti-German tendency of French foreign policy persisted.

The year 1870 revealed more clearly than 1914 what France ultimately intends. Back then, there was no need to conceal the offensive nature of French foreign policy. However, in 1914, perhaps enlightened by experience or influenced by England, it was considered more appropriate to present universal ideals on one side while limiting one's goal to Alsace-Lorraine on the other.

However, these tactical considerations do not in the least indicate an internal departure from France's former goals in foreign policy but only a concealment thereof. The guiding principle of French foreign policy remains the conquest of the Rhine border, viewing the fragmentation of Germany into as many loosely connected individual states as the best protection of this border. Although this achieved European security for France is intended to serve the fulfillment of greater global political goals, it does not change the fact that for Germany, these French continental political intentions are a matter of life and death.

Indeed, France has never participated in any coalition that would have promoted German interests in any way. In the last 300 years, Germany has been invaded by France a total of 29 times until 1870. This fact prompted Bismarck to strongly rebuke French General Wimpffen on the evening of the Battle of Sedan when he attempted to obtain mitigations of the surrender conditions. It was Bismarck who immediately countered Wimpffen's assertion that France would not forget Germany's leniency but would preserve a grateful memory of it in the future. Bismarck pointed out the harsh, naked facts of history, emphasizing that France had attacked Germany so many times in the last 300 years, regardless of which government systems were in power, that he was convinced that no matter how the capitulation was formulated, France would immediately attack Germany again as soon as it felt strong enough to do so, either through its own strength or through the power of alliances.

Bismarck thus assessed the French mentality more accurately than our current political leaders in Germany. He was able to do so because, having his own political goals in mind, he also possessed an understanding of the political objectives of others. For Bismarck, the intention of French foreign policy was clear. However, our present so-called statesmen find it incomprehensible because they themselves lack any clear political thought.

If, incidentally, France had only intended to regain Alsace-Lorraine upon entering the World War, the energy of French warfare would not have been nearly as intense as it was. Especially the political leadership would not have been driven to the resolute action that appears admirable during certain situations throughout the World War. However, it was inherent in the nature of this greatest coalition war of all times that complete fulfillment of all desires was all the less possible, as the internal interests of the nations participating in it had very significant differences. The French desire for the complete obliteration of Germany in Europe always stood opposed to the English desire to prevent not only French but also German unconditional hegemony.

Significant for curtailing French war aims was the fact that the German collapse occurred in forms that initially did not fully bring the magnitude of the catastrophe to public consciousness. In France, the German grenadier had been encountered in such a way that one could only apprehensively anticipate a possibility that might have forced France to pursue its last political goal alone. However, when later, under the impression of the now universally visible internal defeat of Germany, such action would have been determined, the wartime psychosis of the other world had already subsided to such an extent that without contradiction from the previous allies, France could not have carried out a sole action of such great final intentions.

However, this does not mean that France has renounced its goal. On the contrary, it will persistently attempt in the future to achieve what the present prevented. France will continue to strive, as it has always done, to dissolve Germany as soon as it feels capable, either through its own strength or through the power of alliances, and will seek to occupy the Rhine to be able to deploy French power unthreatened at other points. The fact that France is not in the least deterred in its intentions by changes in German forms of government is all the more understandable, as the French people themselves, regardless of their constitutions, consistently adhere to their foreign policy ideas. A people that consistently pursues a specific foreign policy goal regardless of whether it has a republic or a monarchy, a civil democracy, or Jacobin terror ruling the state, will not understand that another people might change its foreign policy goals with changes in its forms of government.

Therefore, France's attitude towards Germany will not change, regardless of whether Germany is represented by an empire or a republic, or even if socialist terror were to dominate the state.

Of course, France is not indifferent to internal German developments, but its attitude will only be determined by the probability of greater success, thus facilitating its foreign policy actions through a specific German form of government. France will desire for Germany the constitution that expects the least resistance from France in the destruction of Germany.

Therefore, when the German Republic, in an attempt to demonstrate its value, cites French friendship, it is actually the most damning indictment against it. Because only then, when it is perceived by France as lacking in value for Germany, is it welcomed in Paris. However, this does not mean that France will treat this German Republic differently than it did analogous weaknesses in our state's existence in past times. At the Seine, German weakness was always loved more than German strength because it seemed to guarantee an easier success of France's foreign policy activities.

This French tendency will not be changed by the fact that the French people do not suffer from a lack of space. For centuries, politics in France has been determined least by purely economic needs, but rather by moments of sentiment. France is a classic example of how the sense of a healthy policy of territorial expansion can easily swing to the opposite when national principles are no longer decisive and are replaced by so-called state-national principles.

French-national chauvinism has distanced itself from ethnic perspectives to the extent that, for the sake of satisfying a pure lust for power, it allows its own blood to be diluted, only to maintain the numerical character of a grand nation. Therefore, France will remain an eternal disturber of the world until a decisive and thorough education of this people takes place. Moreover, no one has characterized the character of French vanity better than Schopenhauer with his statement: "Africa has its apes, and Europe has its French."

From this mixture of vanity and megalomania, French foreign policy has always derived its inner drive. Who in Germany can hope and expect that, as France becomes more estranged from rational clear thinking due to its general blackening, it will one day change its mindset and intentions towards Germany?

No, no matter how the next development in Europe unfolds, France will always attempt, by exploiting German weaknesses and all diplomatic and military means at its disposal, to harm us and divide our people in order to finally bring about its complete dissolution.

Therefore, any European coalition that does not involve binding France is automatically forbidden for Germany.

In itself, the belief in German-Russian reconciliation is fantastical as long as a regime reigns in Russia that is filled with the sole desire to transmit Bolshevik poisoning to Germany. Therefore, when communist elements advocate for a German-Russian alliance, it is natural. They rightfully hope to be able to lead Germany to Bolshevism themselves.

However, it is incomprehensible when national Germans believe they can come to an understanding with a state whose highest interest is the destruction of precisely this national Germany. It is self-evident that if such an alliance were to be definitively established today, its result would be the complete domination of Jewry in Germany just as in Russia. The notion that with this Russia, a fight against the capitalist Western European world could be carried out is also incomprehensible.

Firstly, today's Russia is anything but an anti-capitalist state. It is, however, a country that has destroyed its own national economy but only to grant the international financial capital the opportunity for absolute domination. If this were not the case, then why would a decidedly capitalist world in Germany take a stand in favor of such an alliance? It is the Jewish press organs with the most pronounced stock market interests in Germany that advocate for a German-Russian alliance in one form or another. Does one truly believe that the Berliner Tagblatt or the Frankfurter Zeitung, and all their illustrated publications, speak, in more or less open form, for Bolshevik Russia because it is an anti-capitalist state? It is always a curse when in political matters, desire becomes the father of thought.

However, it would be conceivable that an internal change could occur within Bolshevik Russia, insofar as the Jewish element might be displaced by a more or less Russian national one. Then it would also not be ruled out that today's actually Jewish-capitalist Bolshevik Russia would be driven toward national-anti-capitalist tendencies. In this case, which may seem to be indicated in some respects, it would still be conceivable that Western European capitalism would seriously take a stand against Russia. However, even then, an alliance of Germany with this Russia would be sheer madness. Because the belief that such a pact could be kept secret is just as unfounded as the hope of quietly preparing for the confrontation through military preparations.

There would really be only two possibilities: Either this alliance would be viewed by the Western European world that would then arise against Russia as a danger or not. If yes, then I do not know who seriously believes that we would have the time to arm ourselves adequately to prevent a collapse for at least the first 24 hours. Or does one truly believe that France would wait until we had built up our air defense and tank defense?

Or does one believe that this could happen in secret in a country where betrayal is no longer seen as shameless but as admirable courage? No, if Germany truly wanted to conclude an alliance with Russia against Western Europe today, then Germany would again have become the historical battleground tomorrow. And then it would take a very rare imagination to imagine that Russia could somehow, I don't know by what means, come to our aid.

The only success of such action would be that Russia might escape the catastrophe for a certain time by first breaking out over Germany. However, there could not be a more popular pretext for such a struggle against Germany, especially in the Western states. Imagine Germany allied with a truly anti-capitalist Russia, and then imagine how this democratic world Jewish press would mobilize all the instincts of the other nations against Germany.

How, especially in France, full harmony would be restored immediately between French national chauvinism and the Jewish-stock exchange press. Because one should not confuse such a process with the battles of White Russian generals against Bolshevism back then. In 1919 and 1920, national White Russia fought against the Jewish-stock exchange, truly, in the highest sense, international-capitalist red revolution.

However, today, nationalized anti-capitalist Bolshevism would stand in battle against world Jewry. Anyone who knows the significance of press propaganda, its limitless potential for incitement and dumbing down of people, can imagine the orgies of hate and passion to which the European

Western nations would be whipped up against Germany. Because then Germany would no longer be allied with the Russia of a great, remarkable, ethical, bold idea, but with the despoilers of human civilization.

There could be no better opportunity, especially for the French government, to overcome its own internal difficulties than to engage in a completely risk-free fight against Germany in such a case. French national chauvinism could be all the more satisfied, as then, under the protection of a new world coalition, the fulfillment of the ultimate war goal could be significantly closer. Because regardless of the nature of the alliance between Germany and Russia, Germany would have to bear the most terrible blows militarily on its own.

Apart from the fact that Russia does not directly border Germany and would therefore have to overrun the Polish state itself, even in the event of Poland being subdued by Russia, which in itself is unlikely, such Russian assistance could only arrive on German territory, if there is no Germany left. However, the idea of Russian divisions landing somewhere in Germany is completely out of the question as long as England and France also completely control the Baltic Sea. Moreover, the landing of Russian troops in Germany would fail due to numerous technical deficiencies.

So if a German-Russian alliance were ever to face the test of reality, and there are no alliances without thoughts of war, then Germany would be exposed to the concentric attacks of all of Western Europe without being able to offer any serious resistance of its own.

However, the question remains as to what sense a German-Russian alliance should have at all. Only one sense, to save Russia from destruction and to sacrifice Germany for it? Because no matter how this alliance would end, Germany could not come to a final foreign policy goal. This would not change the fundamental question of life, indeed, the vital necessity of our people. On the contrary, Germany would be even more separated from a single rational land policy, to fill its future with the struggle for insignificant border adjustments. Because neither in the West nor in the South of Europe can the spatial question of our people be solved.

The hope for a German-Russian alliance, which also haunts the minds of many national German politicians, is also more than doubtful for another reason.

In general, it seems self-evident in national circles that one cannot ally oneself with a Jewish-Bolshevik Russia, since the result would most likely be the Bolshevization of Germany itself. It is obvious that one does not want this. However, one's hope is based on the belief that one day the Jewish and thus fundamentally international capitalist character of Bolshevism would disappear in Russia, to make room for a national world anti-capitalist communism. This Russia, then filled with national tendencies again, would indeed be suitable for entering into a federal relationship with Germany.

This is a very great mistake. It is based on the extraordinary ignorance of the psyche of the Slavic national soul. It should not surprise one, considering how little knowledge even politicized Germany had of the mental states of its former allies. Otherwise, one would never have fallen so deeply. If these Russia-friendly national politicians today try to motivate their politics by referring to Bismarck's analogous attitudes, then they disregard a whole host of important factors that spoke in favor of a Russia-friendly policy at that time, but are now against it.

The Russia that Bismarck knew, at least as far as its political leadership was concerned, was not a typical Slavic state. Slavic peoples in general lack state-building forces. Particularly in Russia, state formations have always been managed by foreign elements. Since the time of Peter the Great, it was primarily many Germans who formed the backbone and brain of the Russian state. Over the centuries, countless thousands of these Germans have been Russified, but only in the sense that our bourgeoisie, our nationalities, Poles, and Czechs, want to Germanize or Germanize them.

Just as in this case, the newly made German is in truth only a German-speaking Pole or Czech, these artificial Russians have remained Germanic in blood and therefore in their abilities, or rather Germanic. Russia owed its state existence, as well as the few existing cultural values, to this Germanic upper and intellectual class. Without this genuinely Germanic upper class, neither would a Great Russia have emerged, nor could it have maintained itself.

As long as Russia was a state with autocratic forms of government, this non-Russian upper class in reality also decisively influenced the political life of the giant empire. And at least partly, this Russia was also known to Bismarck. The reliability, especially from Russia, and stability of Russian politics, both domestically and internationally, had already begun to falter and become partially unpredictable during his lifetime.

This was due to the slow displacement of the Germanic upper class. This process of transforming Russian intelligence was partly due to a depletion of the Russian national body as a result of numerous wars, which, as mentioned in this book, primarily decimated the racially more valuable forces. In fact, especially the officer corps was by descent mostly non-Slavic, but in any case not of Russian blood.

Added to this was the lower reproduction rate of the upper intelligence classes themselves, and finally the artificial elevation of a truly blood-related Russian nationality through schools. The low state-preserving value of the new Russian intelligence itself was blood-related and perhaps showed itself most sharply in the nihilism of the Russian university system. But at its deepest core, this nihilism was nothing more than the blood-related opposition of true Russianhood to the racially foreign upper class.

In proportion as the Germanic state-building upper class of Russia was replaced by a racially purely Russian bourgeois class, the pan-Slavic idea confronted the Russian state idea. It was from its inception, both racially Russian-Slavic and anti-German. However, the anti-German sentiment of the newly forming Russian nation, especially in the so-called intelligentsia, was not just a pure reflex movement against the previous autocratic foreign upper class in Russia, arising from politically liberal ideas, but rather in the innermost sense, the protest of the Slavic essence against the German.

These are two national souls that have very little in common, and it would even have to be determined whether this little in common has its cause in the mixed racial individual elements from which both the Russian and German peoples appear to be composed. Thus, what is common to us Germans and the Russians does not correspond to either the German or Russian character, but is only attributable to our racial mixture, which brought both East Slavic and Slavic elements to Germany, as well as Nordic-German elements to Russia.

But if one were to take a purely Nordic German, say from Westphalia, and juxtapose him with a purely Slavic Russian, then an infinite gulf would open up between these two representatives of two peoples. In fact, the Slavic-Russian people have always felt this and therefore always had an instinctive aversion to the German. The hard thoroughness as well as the cold logic, the sober thinking are inwardly unsympathetic to the real Russian and partly also incomprehensible.

Our sense of order will not only find no reciprocation but will always evoke aversion. What is felt by us as self-evident is thus a torment for the Russian, as it represents a restriction of his natural, differently structured soul and instinctive life. Hence, Slavic Russia will always feel more drawn to France.

And to an increasing extent, as the Frankish-Nordic element is also pushed back in France. The light, superficial, more or less feminine French life is more able to captivate the Slav because it is more inwardly related to him than the harshness of our German struggle for existence. It is therefore no coincidence that politically pan-Slavic Russia was enthusiastic about France, just as the Russian intelligentsia of Slavic blood found Paris to be the Mecca of its own civilizational needs.

The process of the rise of a Russian national bourgeoisie at the same time meant an inner alienation of this new Russia from Germany, which could no longer rely on a racially related Russian upper class in the future. In fact, the anti-German attitude of the representatives of the racial pan-Slavic idea was already so strong around the turn of the century, and its influence on Russian politics had grown so much, that even Germany's more than decent attitude towards Russia during the Russo-Japanese War could no longer stop the further alienation of the two states. The World War came, which had also been fueled to no small extent by pan-Slavic agitation. The real state Russia, as it had been represented by the previous upper class, hardly had a say in it anymore.

The World War itself brought about a further depletion of Russia from Nordic-German elements, and the last remnants were finally eradicated by the revolution and Bolshevism. Not as if the Slavic racial instinct alone consciously carried out the struggle of extermination against the previous non-Russian upper class. No, it has meanwhile received its new leader in Judaism. Judaism, pushing after the upper class and thus the upper leadership, eradicated the previous foreign upper class with the help of Slavic racial instincts. Because if with the Bolshevik revolution Judaism took over leadership in all areas of Russian life, this is a natural process, for in itself and from itself, Slavdom entirely lacks any organizational ability and therefore any state-building and state-preserving power. Remove all non-Slavic elements from Slavdom and it will immediately fall into a state of dissolution.

However, fundamentally, every state formation may have its innermost cause in the encounter between peoples of higher and lower order, with those bearing the higher value of blood developing a certain sense of community for reasons of self-preservation, which only allows them the possibility of organization and domination of the inferior. Only overcoming common tasks compels organizational forms. However, the difference between state-building and non-state-building elements lies precisely in the fact that the former are enabled to shape an organization for the preservation of their kind against other beings, while the non-state-building are incapable of finding on their own those organizational forms that would ensure their existence against others.

Thus, today's Russia, or rather the present Slavdom of Russian nationality, has obtained Judaism as its mistress, which initially eliminated the previous upper class and would now have to prove its own state-building power. However, given the entirely destructive disposition of Judaism, it will only act here as the historical ferment of decomposition. It has called upon spirits that it itself will no longer be able to rid itself of, and the struggle of the internally anti-state pan-Slavic idea against the Bolshevik Jewish state idea will end with the destruction of Judaism.

But what remains will be a Russia with as little state power as deeply ingrained anti-German sentiment. Since this state will not possess any more firmly rooted state-preserving upper class, it will become a source of eternal unrest and eternal insecurity. A gigantic territory will thus be exposed to the most varied fate, and instead of stabilizing the state of affairs on Earth, a period of restless changes will begin.

The first phase of these developments will be that the various nations of the world will attempt to establish relations with this vast state complex, in order to bring about a strengthening of their own positions and intentions in this way. However, such an attempt will always be bound to the endeavor to exert its own intellectual and organizational influence on Russia in the process.

Germany must not hope to be somehow involved in this development. The entire mentality of present and future Russia is opposed to it. Neither from the standpoint of sober expediency, nor from that of human solidarity, does an alliance between Germany and Russia make sense for Germany in the future. On the contrary, it is fortunate for the future that this development has occurred, because it has broken a spell that would have prevented us from seeking the goal of German foreign policy where it can only lie: space in the East.

—————————————— 19 ——————————————

CHAPTER 12
Principles of German Foreign Policy

—————————————— 28 ——————————————

Considering the hopeless military situation of Germany, the following must be taken into account in shaping the future German foreign policy:

1. Germany cannot, on its own, bring about a change in its current situation if this change would have to be achieved through military means.

2. Germany cannot hope that measures by the League of Nations will change its situation as long as the dominant representatives of this institution are also interested in Germany's destruction.

3. Germany cannot hope to change its current situation through a coalition of powers that would put it in conflict with the French alliance system spanning Germany, without Germany first having the opportunity to address its purely military impotence in order to be able to appear militarily successful in the event of the application of alliance obligations.

4. Germany cannot hope to find such a coalition of powers until its final foreign policy goal is clearly defined and does not contradict the interests of those states that could come into consideration for an alliance with Germany, but even appears to serve them.

5. Germany cannot hope that these states can be ones outside the League of Nations; on the contrary, its only hope must be that it succeeds in breaking out of the existing coalition of victorious states and forming a new group of interested parties with new goals, the realization of which fundamentally cannot take place within the framework of the League of Nations.

6. Germany can only hope to succeed in this way if it definitively abandons its previous wavering policy of oscillation and fundamentally decides on a direction and assumes and bears all the consequences thereof.

7. Germany should never hope to be able to make world history by forming alliances with peoples whose military value either appears sufficiently marked by the fact of their previous defeat or whose general racial significance is inferior, for the struggle for the restoration of German freedom will thus elevate German history again to world history.

8. Germany should never forget for a moment that, no matter how or by what means it intends to change its fate, France will be its opponent, and that any coalition of powers that turns against Germany can count on France's support from the outset.

---------- 19 ----------

CHAPTER 13
Possible Goals

---------- 28 ----------

One cannot assess Germany's foreign policy possibilities without first having clarity about what Germany itself wants, how Germany intends to shape its future. Furthermore, one must attempt to clarify the foreign policy goals of those powers in Europe that, as members of the victorious coalition, have the significance of world powers.

I have already discussed the various foreign policy possibilities for Germany in this book. However, I want to briefly outline the possible foreign policy goals once again, so that they provide a basis for critically examining the circumstances of these individual foreign policy goals in relation to those of other European states.

1

Germany can completely dispense with a fundamental foreign policy goal. This essentially means it can decide on anything and does not need to commit to anything.

Continuing the policy of the last 30 years under different circumstances in the future. If the world consisted solely of states with similar political aimlessness, this could be tolerated, if not justified, for Germany. However, this is not the case. Just as in ordinary life, a person with a clear life goal that they strive to achieve under all circumstances will always be superior to aimless others, so too in the life of nations. This does not at all mean that a state without political goals will be able to avoid the dangers that such a situation might bring. As much as it may seem relieved of active activity due to its own political aimlessness, it can easily become the victim of the political goals of others in its passivity. Because a state's actions are not only determined by its own will but also by that of others, with the difference that in one case, it can determine the law of action itself, while in the other case, it is imposed upon it. Not wanting a war out of a peaceful disposition does not mean one can necessarily avoid it. And wanting to avoid a war at all costs does not necessarily mean saving life from death.

Germany's position in Europe today is such that, even with its own political aimlessness, it cannot hope to proceed toward a state of contemplative tranquility. Such a possibility does not exist for a people located in the heart of Europe. Either Germany attempts to actively participate in shaping life, or it will be a passive object of the life-shaping of other peoples. All the wisdom that previously thought it could extract peoples from historical dangers through declarations of general disinterest has always proven to be as cowardly as it is foolish. Those who do not want to be a hammer in history will be an anvil. Our German people have always had to choose between these two possibilities in their entire history. When it wanted to make history itself, it gladly and boldly engaged itself accordingly, and it was still the hammer. But if it believed it could renounce the obligations of the struggle for life, then it has always been the anvil on which others fought their struggle for life, or it served as food for foreigners.

Therefore, if Germany wants to live, it must take on the defense of this life, and the best defense has always been the blow. Indeed, Germany cannot hope to do anything for its own life if it does not muster a clear foreign policy goal that appears suitable to bring the German struggle for life into wise relation to the interests of other peoples.

However, if this is not done, aimlessness on a large scale will lead to lack of planning in detail. This lack of planning will gradually turn us into a second Poland in Europe. In the same measure that we become weaker thanks to our general political defeatism and the only activity of our life then only finds expression in domestic politics, we will sink politically into a plaything of world-historical events, the motivating forces of which arise from the life and interest struggles of other peoples.

Furthermore, peoples who are unable to make a clear decision about their own future and therefore prefer not to participate in the game of world development are perceived by all players as spoilsports and equally hated. Indeed, it may even happen that the lack of planning in individual political actions, which is based on general political aimlessness, is perceived as a very sophisticated and opaque game and is accordingly answered. This was one of the misfortunes that befell us in the pre-war period. The more opaque and incomprehensible the political decisions of the German government of the time were, the more suspicious they seemed, and the more one detected behind even the most foolish steps thoughts of a particularly dangerous nature.

Therefore, if Germany today does not muster a clear political goal, it practically forfeits all possibilities for a revision of our current fate, without being able to avoid further dangers for the future in the least.

2

Germany aims to continue its economic activities peacefully, as it has done so far, to ensure the sustenance of the German people. Accordingly, it intends to play a leading role in world industry, export, and trade in the future. It seeks to rebuild a substantial merchant fleet, establish coal stations and bases in other parts of the world, and ultimately secure not only international markets but also its own sources of raw materials, preferably in the form of colonies. Such a development in the future will inevitably need to be protected, particularly through maritime means of power.

However, this entire political goal for the future is utopian unless England is subdued beforehand. It resurrects all the reasons that led to the World War in 1914. Any attempt by Germany to rebuild its past through this path will end in mortal enmity with England, with France being considered the surest partner from the outset.

From a national standpoint, this foreign policy objective is ominous, and from a realpolitik perspective, it is insane.

3

Germany sets the restoration of the borders of 1914 as its foreign policy goal.

However, this goal is insufficient from a national standpoint, unsatisfactory from a military perspective, impossible from a future-oriented nationalist viewpoint, and insane considering its consequences. By pursuing this objective, Germany would face the entire former coalition of victors as a unified front of adversaries in the future. Given our current military situation, which will deteriorate year by year if the present state persists, how to restore the old borders remains an impenetrable mystery to our national and patriotic statesmen.

4

Germany decides to adopt a clear and far-sighted spatial policy as its future goal. It thereby departs from all attempts at global industrial and trade policies and instead concentrates all its efforts on delineating a sufficient living space for our people for the next 100 years. Since this space can only be found in the East, the obligation to become a naval power takes a back seat. Germany once again endeavors to defend its interests by striving to become a decisive land power.

This goal aligns with the highest national and ethnic demands. It also requires significant military capabilities for implementation but does not necessarily bring Germany into conflict with all European powers. While France will remain Germany's adversary, such a foreign policy goal provides little reason for England and especially Italy to maintain the enmity of the World War.

---------- 19 ----------

CHAPTER 14
Germany & England

---------- 28 ----------

For a closer understanding of the possibilities mentioned here, it is appropriate to consider the major foreign policy goals of the other European powers. These goals are partly discernible from the past activities and effectiveness of these states, partly explicitly laid out programmatically, and partly dictated by necessities so clear that even if these states temporarily pursue other paths, the force of harsh reality would compel them to return to these goals.

The fact that England has a clear foreign policy objective is evidenced by the existence and emergence of this giant empire. One cannot imagine forging a world empire without a clear will to do so. It is natural that not every individual of such a people goes to work every day with thoughts of the grand foreign policy objectives, but slowly, an entire nation becomes seized by such objectives, so that even the unconscious actions of individuals align with the general trajectory of these objectives and actually contribute to them. Even in the character of such a people, the general political goal gradually takes shape, and the pride of today's Englishman is nothing but the pride of the ancient Roman. The notion that world empires owe their emergence to chance or that at least the events that led to their construction were random historical processes that always turned out favorably for a people is false. Ancient Rome owed its greatness just as much as present-day England to the correctness of Moltke's assertion that in the long run, luck favors only the capable. However, the capability of a people lies not only in racial value but also in the ability and skill with which these values are utilized. A world empire the size of ancient Rome or present-day Great Britain is always the result of a marriage of the highest national value and the clearest political objective. If one of these factors begins to falter, weakness ensues, and perhaps even decline.

The objective of present-day England is determined by the inherent value of the Anglo-Saxon people and their insular location. It was inherent in the value of the Anglo-Saxon people to strive for space. Inevitably, this drive could only find fulfillment outside of present-day Europe.

Not that the English did not also attempt, from time to time, to satisfy their expansionist desires in Europe; however, all these undertakings failed because they faced states of at least equal racial merit at the time. The later English expansion into the so-called colonies led from the outset to an extraordinary increase in English maritime life. It is interesting to see how England, initially exporting people, finally transitions to exporting goods and thereby even reduces its own agriculture. Although a large part of today's English people, indeed, the average, falls below the highest German value, centuries of tradition have so deeply ingrained this people that it possesses significant political advantages over our German people. While the Earth now possesses an English world empire, there is currently no other people better equipped due to its general political characteristics and average political sagacity.

The fundamental idea that governed English colonial policy was, on the one hand, to find markets for English manpower and to maintain them in a state relationship with the motherland, and on the other hand, to secure markets and sources of raw materials for the English economy. It is understandable that the English are convinced that Germans cannot colonize, just as it is understandable that Germans believe the same about the English. Both peoples take different positions when assessing their colonization capabilities. The English approach was infinitely practical and sober, while the German one was more romantic.

When Germany sought its first colonies, it was already a military state and thus a major power. It had earned the title of a world power through enduring achievements in all areas of human culture as well as military prowess. It was noteworthy that particularly in the 19th century, there was a general trend toward colonies among all peoples, although the originally guiding idea had already completely vanished. Germany, for example, justified its claim to colonies with its ability and desire to spread German culture.

This is nonsense. Because you cannot convey culture, which is a general expression of life of a specific people, to any other people with completely different mental prerequisites. This would only be possible with a so-called international civilization, which, however, relates to culture as jazz music does to a Beethoven symphony.

But aside from that, it would never have occurred to an Englishman at the time of founding the English colonies to motivate his actions other than with very real and sober advantages that they would bring. If later England advocated for freedom of the seas or for oppressed nations, it was never to justify its own colonization activities, but only to destroy unpleasant competitors. Hence, English colonial activities had to be partly very successful for the most natural reasons. Because the less the Englishman thought about imposing English culture or civilization on the savages, who were absolutely not hungry for culture, the more sympathetic such rule must have appeared to the absolutely uncultured savage.

Additionally, there was the whip, which could also be applied all the more easily, as there was never any danger of contradicting a cultural mission. England needed markets and sources of raw materials for its goods. And it secured these markets through power politics.

That is the essence of English colonial policy. However, despite this, England also mentioned the word "culture" later on, but only from purely agitational viewpoints, to be able to morally embellish its own so sober actions. In reality, the inner living conditions of the savages were completely irrelevant to the English for as long and to such an extent as they did not affect the living conditions of the English themselves.

That with colonies the size of India, other notions of prestige politics were associated, is understandable and comprehensible. But it can never be denied that English interests determine the living conditions in India, not vice versa. And it is also not disputable that in India, the English do not establish any cultural institutions so that the native may partake in English culture, but rather that at most the Englishman can benefit more from his colonies and facilitate their better exploitation and easier domination.

Or does one believe that England brought railways to India only to provide the Indians with European means of transportation, and not to enable better utilization of the colony and to guarantee easier domination through them?

When today England in Egypt once again follows the footsteps of the Pharaohs and stores up the Nile with gigantic dams, then surely not to ease the earthly existence of the poor fellah, but only to make English cotton independent of the American monopoly. However, these are all perspectives that Germany dared to openly consider in its colonial policy. The English were educators of the natives for England's interests, and the German was the teacher. That at the end the natives may have felt more comfortable with us than under the English would not speak for our, but rather for the English style of colonization policy, according to a normal Englishman.

This policy of gradual world conquest, in which economic power and political strength always went hand in hand, determined England's position towards other states. The more England grew into its colonial power, the more it needed control over the seas, and the more it gained control over the seas, the more it became a colonial power again, but also the more jealous it became to ensure that no one challenged its control of the seas or possession of colonies.

In Germany, there is a widespread and very mistaken notion that England immediately opposes any European hegemony. This is actually incorrect. England has always paid little attention to European affairs as long as no potential world competitor emerged from them, viewing any threat only in a development that could eventually disrupt its maritime and colonial dominance.

There is no European conflict in which England has not defended its trade and overseas interests. The conflicts against Spain, Holland, and later France were not rooted in the threatening military power of these states per se, but rather in the manner of their foundation and the impact thereof. If Spain had not been a transatlantic competitor of England, it would likely have paid little attention to Spain.

The same goes for Holland. And even England's later gigantic struggle against France was not waged against a continental France of Napoleon's, but against the Napoleonic France, which viewed its continental policy only as a springboard and base for larger, not necessarily continental goals. Ultimately, the most threatening power to England due to its geographical location was France. It was perhaps the only state where even a certain continental development could pose future dangers to England. However, it is all the more remarkable and instructive for us Germans that England nevertheless decided to join forces with France in the World War.

Instructive because it proves that despite adhering to the great fundamental principles of English foreign policy, there, they always count on the available possibilities and never relinquish them simply because at some point in the nearer or more distant future, they might pose a threat to England. Our German God-punish-England politicians always believe that a good relationship with England in the future must fail because England does not seriously consider promoting Germany through an alliance with it, only to face it again one day as a threatening power. Of course, England will not enter into an alliance to promote Germany but only to promote British interests.

However, England has provided numerous examples that the representation of its interests has often been coupled with the representation of the interests of other peoples, and that it has resorted to alliances, even though human foresight predicted that these might turn into later enmity. Because ultimately, political marriages always lead to earlier or later divorce, as they do not serve a common representation of interests of both parties, but only want to protect or promote the currently not opposing interests of two states with common means.

That England does not fundamentally oppose a European great power of overwhelming military significance as long as the foreign policy goals of this power are evidently purely continental in nature is evidenced by its behavior towards Prussia. Or does anyone want to deny that under Frederick the Great,

Prussia's military power was by far the strongest in Europe? Don't believe that England did not fight against Prussia at that time only because, despite its military hegemony, it had to be considered one of the smaller states in Europe in terms of spatial size.

Absolutely not.

Because when England once fought its battles against the Dutch, the territorial extent of the Dutch state in Europe was still significantly smaller than that of late-Frederician Prussia, and one could not speak of a threatening hegemony or dominance of Holland in Europe at all. However, if Prussia had not exclusively devoted itself to purely continental goals, England would have considered it its fiercest enemy at all times, regardless of the size of Prussia's purely military means in Europe or the danger of European hegemony by Prussia.

Our less-thinking national-patriotic politicians often bitterly accuse the successors of the Great Elector of neglecting the overseas possessions of Prussia initiated by the Great Elector, indeed abandoning them altogether, and thus having no interests in maintaining and expanding a Brandenburg-Prussian fleet. It is fortunate for Prussia and for later Germany that this was the case.

Nothing speaks more for outstanding statecraft, especially that of Friedrich Wilhelm I, than his concentration of the modest resources of the small Prussian state, despite all frugality, solely on the promotion of the land army. Not only did this enable the small state to attain a superior position in one weapon, but it also spared it from the enmity of England. A Prussia following in Holland's footsteps would not have been able to fight the three Silesian Wars with England also as an adversary.

Apart from the fact that any attempt to achieve real maritime dominance for the small Prussian state would have inevitably failed in the long run due to the extremely limited and militarily unfavorable territorial base of the homeland. It would have been child's play for the English even then to rid themselves of the dangerous competitor in Europe through a general coalition war. That Brandenburg could ever become the later Prussia and the later Prussia a new German Reich was solely due to that wise insight into the real balance of power and the possibilities of Prussia at the time, with which the Hohenzollerns restricted themselves almost exclusively to strengthening the land forces until the Bismarckian era. It was the only clear, consistent policy.

If German-Prussia and later Germany wanted to face a future at all, it could only be guaranteed by a land supremacy equivalent to England's at sea. It was a misfortune for Germany that it slowly deviated from this realization, inadequately developed land-based power, and instead turned to a naval policy that ultimately amounted to no more than half measures. Even the Germany of the post-Bismarckian period could not afford the luxury of creating and maintaining superior armaments on land and at sea simultaneously. However, it is one of the most important principles for all times that a people recognize the most indispensably necessary weapon for the preservation of their existence and then promote it to the utmost using all means.

England has recognized and followed this. For England, maritime supremacy was truly the be-all and end-all of its existence. Even the most brilliant military periods on the continent, glorious wars, incomparable military decisions, could not persuade the English to regard anything ultimately subordinate in the land forces for England, and to concentrate the entire strength of the nation on maintaining superior maritime dominance.

In Germany, however, one was swept away by the great colonial wave of the nineteenth century, perhaps also strengthened by romantic memories of the old Hanseatic League, as well as driven by the economically peaceful policy, to postpone the exclusive promotion of the land army and to initiate the construction of a fleet. This policy then found its final expression in the equally mistaken and ominous phrase: Our future lies on the water.

No, quite the contrary, for us it lay and lies in Europe on land, just as the causes of our downfall will always be purely continental in nature: Our unhappy spatially and militarily geographical terrible situation.

As long as Prussia confined its foreign policy ambitions to purely European goals, it had no serious dangers to fear from England. The objection that, nevertheless, there was a pro-French sentiment in England as early as

1870/71 is not accurate and, in any case, does not signify anything. For at that time, there was also a pro-German sentiment in England, and even in English churches, France's actions were denounced as a sin. Furthermore, the actually adopted official stance decides. It is quite natural that in a state of England's importance, France will have ongoing sympathies, especially as the influence on a country's press is often exercised by foreign capital.

France has always managed to mobilize sympathies for itself in a very clever manner. Its most excellent auxiliary weapon in this regard has always been Paris. But this did not happen only in England, but even in Germany.

In the midst of the war in 1870/71, there was even a not insignificant clique in Berlin society, even at the Berlin court, that did not hide its pro-French sympathies, and managed to delay the bombardment of Paris for some time. Moreover, it is humanly understandable that English circles looked with mixed pleasure at the German military successes. Their official stance could not, in any case, prompt them to intervene.

The opinion that this can only be attributed to Russian support, which Bismarck had secured, does not change this. For this support was primarily intended against Austria. However, if England had abandoned its neutral stance at that time, even Russian support would not have been able to prevent a comprehensive conflagration.

Because then Austria would have certainly reappeared, and one way or another, the success of 1871 would hardly have occurred. In fact, Bismarck had an ongoing quiet fear of the interference of other states, not only in the war but even in the peace negotiations. For what happened later with Russia, the intervention of other powers could just as easily have been orchestrated by England against Germany.

The change in the English attitude towards Germany can be precisely tracked. It parallels our development at sea, intensifying with our colonial activities to open aversion and finally ending with our naval policy in open hatred. However, it cannot be taken amiss by a truly concerned state leadership that in this development of such an efficient people as the Germans, a threatening danger for the future is perceived in England.

One should never use our German omissions as a yardstick for judging the actions of others. The recklessness with which the Germany of the post-Bismarckian era allowed its power-political position in Europe to be threatened by France and Russia without taking any serious action against it does not allow us to expect similar things from or to break the staff over them in moral indignation when they better represent the vital interests of their peoples. If the Germany of the pre-war period had decided instead of its world peace and economic policies with their inherently disastrous repercussions to continue the former Prussian continental policy, then it could have firstly truly elevated its land forces to that outstanding level that the Prussian state once had, and then it would not have had to fear unconditional enmity with England.

Because it is certain that if Germany had used all the immense resources it poured into the navy to strengthen its land forces, then its interests would have been defended differently on the decisive European battlefields, and the nation would have been spared the fate of slowly bleeding to death with a partly insufficiently equipped land army facing an overwhelming world coalition, while the navy, at least in its decisive combat units in the ports, rusted away, only to finally end its existence in a more than ignominious surrender. Don't make excuses for the leaders, but have the courage to admit that this lay in the nature of this weapon for ourselves.

For at the same time, the field army was thrown out of one battle into another, without regard for losses or other hardships. The land army was truly the German weapon, grown out of a 100-year tradition, but our navy, in the end, was only a romantic whim, a showpiece created for its own sake and again not to be used for its own sake. The overall benefit it brought us is in no proportion to the terrible enmity it brought upon us.

If Germany had not taken this development, then around the turn of the century, it could have reached an understanding with England, which was then willing to negotiate. However, such an understanding could have lasted only if it had been accompanied by a fundamental change in our foreign policy objectives. Even around the turn of the century, Germany could have decided to resume its former Prussian continental policy and jointly dictate further developments in world history with England.

The objection of our eternal hesitators and doubters, that this would have been uncertain, is based on nothing but personal opinions. In any case, English history so far speaks against it. With what right does such a doubter assume that Germany could not have played the same role as Japan did? The foolish phrase that Germany would have then simply been helping the English out of the fire could just as well be applied to Frederick the Great, who ultimately also helped ease the non-European English confrontation with France on the European battlefields.

Furthermore, the further objection that England would have eventually turned against Germany is almost foolish to mention. Because even in that case, Germany's position after the defeat of Russia in Europe would have been better than it was at the beginning of the World War. On the contrary, if the Russo-Japanese War had been fought in Europe between Germany and Russia, then Germany would have gained such a purely moral increase in power that for the next 30 years, any further European power would have thought twice about breaking the peace and rushing into a coalition against Germany. But all these objections always stem from the mentality of pre-war Germany, which, even as the opposition, knew everything and did nothing.

The fact is that back then, approaches were made to Germany from England, and it is also a fact that from the German side, due to the mentality of these eternal hesitating doubters, no clear position could be taken. What Germany rejected at that time, Japan then took care of and relatively cheaply gained the glory of a world power.

However, if in Germany, one did not want to do this under any circumstances, then one would have had to align with the other side. The year 1904 or 05 could have been used for a confrontation with France, with Russia at the back. But even this was as little desired by these hesitators and doubters. Out of pure caution and pure apprehensiveness, and with all their knowledge, they never managed to determine what they actually wanted. And therein lies the superiority of the English government, that they were not governed by such know-it-alls who could never muster the courage to act, but by very naturally thinking people, for whom politics is indeed an art of the possible, but who then also seize all opportunities and truly make use of them.

However, once Germany had evaded such a fundamental understanding with England, which, as already mentioned, would have only made sense in Berlin with a clear spatial-political continental objective, England began to organize world resistance against the threat to British maritime interests.

The World War itself did not go as initially thought, given the military prowess of our people, which was not even suspected in England. Germany was indeed eventually defeated, but only after the American Union appeared on the battlefield, and Germany finally lost the support of its homeland due to its internal collapse. However, the actual English war aim had not been achieved.

While the German threat to English maritime dominance was eliminated, the substantially stronger American threat took its place. In the future, the greatest danger to England will no longer be in Europe but in North America. In Europe itself, the state currently most dangerous to England is France.

Its military hegemony has a particularly threatening significance for England due to the geographical position France occupies in relation to England. Not only do a large part of important English centers appear almost defenseless against French air attacks, but even a number of English cities can be reached by long-range guns from the French coast. Indeed, if modern technology succeeds in significantly increasing the firing capabilities of the heaviest long-range guns, even shelling London from the French mainland would not be beyond the realm of possibility. More importantly, however, a French submarine war against England has a much different basis than the former German one during the World War. France's broad positioning between two seas would make blockade measures, which could easily be successful against the limited wet triangle, much more difficult to implement.

Whoever in today's Europe tries to find natural adversaries of England will always come across France and - Russia. France as a power with continental political goals, which in reality have always been only a backing for very far-reaching general global political intentions. Russia as a threatening enemy of India and owner of oil wells, which today have the same significance as iron and coal mines did in the past century.

If England remains true to its great global political goals, then its potential opponents in Europe, France and Russia, in the rest of the world in the future, will particularly be the American Union.

There is no reason for England to perpetuate its enmity towards Germany. Otherwise, English foreign policy would now be determined by motives that are far from all real logic and might only have a decisive influence on the determination of the political relations between peoples in the mind of a German professor. No, in the future, just as in the past 300 years, England will make its attitudes based on pure expediency, just as it has done for 300 years.

And just as for 300 years, allies of England could become enemies and enemies could become allies again, so it will always be in the future, as long as general and specific necessities speak for it. However, if Germany comes to a fundamental political reorientation that no longer contradicts the maritime and trade interests of England but is exhausted in continental goals, then a logical reason for English enmity, which would then only be enmity for the sake of enmity, no longer exists. For England, the European balance of power is only of interest as long as it prevents the emergence of a world trading and maritime power that is threatening to England. There is no foreign policy leadership less determined by unrealistic doctrines than the English. An empire is not built through sentimental or purely theoretical politics.

Therefore, in the future, the sober perception of British interests will continue to be decisive for English foreign policy. Whoever thwarts these interests will also be England's enemy in the future. Those who do not affect them, their existence will not affect England either. And those who can be useful to them from time to time will be welcomed by England without regard to whether they were previously an enemy and may become one again in the future.

To reject a useful alliance because it might end in enmity later on is something only a bourgeois-national German politician can do. To expect such a thing from an Englishman is an insult to the political instincts of this people.

If, of course, Germany fails to come to any political goals and thus continues to stumble forward without any guiding thought from day to day, or if this goal-setting lies in the restoration of the borders and ownership structures of the year 1914, and thus ultimately ends up again with our world trade, colonial, and maritime power policy, then indeed English enmity towards us will be assured for the future. Then Germany will economically suffocate under its Dawes burdens, politically degenerate under its Locarno treaties, racially weaken itself more and more, only to finally end its existence as a second Holland and a second Switzerland in Europe.

Our bourgeois-national and patriotic politicians can already achieve this; all they need to do is continue on their path of current rhetoric, hurl protests out of their mouths, engage in battles across Europe, and cowardly crawl into a hole before taking any action. They call this national-bourgeois patriotic policy the resurrection of Germany. Just as our bourgeoisie has managed to degrade and compromise the concept of national over the course of barely 60 years, it will also destroy the beautiful concept of patriotic in its downfall by reducing it to a mere phrase within its associations.

However, another important factor comes into play for England's stance towards Germany: the world Jewry, which also holds significant influence in England.

As surely as the English will be able to overcome the war psychosis towards Germany themselves, so surely will world Jewry spare no effort to keep old enmities alive, to prevent the satisfaction of Europe, and to allow its Bolshevik subversion tendencies to take hold in the midst of general unrest.

One cannot speak about world politics without taking this most formidable power into account. Therefore, I will devote special attention to this problem in this book.

---- 19 ----

CHAPTER 15
Germany & Italy

---- 28 ----

If England is not compelled to maintain its enmity towards Germany forever for principled reasons, then even less so is Italy. Italy is the second state in Europe that doesn't fundamentally have to be at odds with Germany; indeed, its foreign policy goals may not even need to conflict with those of Germany. On the contrary, Germany may have more common interests with Italy than with any other state, and vice versa.

During the same period when Germany sought to achieve a new national unity, the same process was occurring in Italy. However, the Italians lacked a central power of gradually increasing and ultimately overwhelming significance, as the emerging Germany had in Prussia. But similar to how France and Austria were real enemies in the way of German unification, the Italian unification movement also suffered most under these two powers.

However, it was mainly the Habsburg state that had a vital interest in maintaining the internal disunity of Italy and indeed possessed it. Since a state of Austria-Hungary's size without direct access to the sea is scarcely conceivable, and the only region suitable for this was at least inhabited by Italians in its cities, Austria had to oppose the creation of a united Italian state out of fear of possible loss of these territories. At that time, even the boldest political goal of the Italian people could only lie in their national unity. This had to then also determine their foreign policy stance.

Therefore, as the Italian unification slowly took shape, its brilliant statesman Cavour utilized all possible means that could serve this particular purpose. Italy owes the possibility of its unification to an extraordinarily wisely chosen alliance policy. The primary goal was always to paralyze the main adversary of this unification, Austria-Hungary, and finally to persuade this state to leave the northern Italian provinces.

Thus, even after the conclusion of the provisional unification of Italy, over 800,000 Italians remained alone in Austria-Hungary. The national goal of further uniting people of Italian nationality had to be postponed, as for the first time the dangers of an Italian-French alienation began to arise. Italy decided to enter the Triple Alliance, especially to buy time for its internal consolidation.

The World War finally brought Italy, for reasons I have already mentioned, into the camp of the Entente. Italian unification has thus taken a huge step forward, but it is still not complete today. However, the greatest event for the Italian state is the elimination of the hated Habsburg Empire. However, a South Slavic entity takes its place, which from a general national perspective poses scarcely less of a threat to Italy.

Just as a purely bourgeois-national, purely border-political conception could not permanently satisfy the life needs of our people in Germany, so too could the purely bourgeois-national unification policy of the Italian state not satisfy the Italian people. Like the German people, the Italian people live on too small and in part infertile dead land. This overpopulation has forced Italy into a permanent emigration for many decades, indeed probably for centuries.

Although a large part of these emigrants return to Italy as seasonal workers to live off their savings, this only led to a further exacerbation of the situation. The population problem was thus not only not solved but exacerbated. Just as Germany became dependent on the capacity, the possibility, and the willingness of other powers and countries to absorb its exports, so too did Italy with its emigration. In both cases, any stoppage of the receiving markets due to events would lead to catastrophic consequences internally.

Italy's attempt to solve the food problem by increasing its industrial activity cannot therefore lead to a definitive success because the lack of natural resources in the motherland Italy deprives it of a large degree of the necessary competitiveness from the outset. Just as in Italy, the conceptions of a formal bourgeois national policy are overcome and instead a sense of national responsibility emerges, this state will also be forced to depart from its previous political conception to turn to a generous spatial policy.

The natural area of Italian expansion remains the peripheral basin of the Mediterranean Sea. The more present-day Italy deviates from its previous national unification policy toward imperialism, the more it will follow the paths of ancient Rome, not out of arrogance, but out of deep internal necessities. If Germany seeks land in Eastern Europe today, it is not a sign of exaggerated power hunger but merely the consequence of its need for territory. Similarly, if Italy seeks to expand its influence on the periphery of the Mediterranean basin and eventually establish colonies, it is also just the result of a natural representation of interests prompted by circumstances. If the German policy before the war had not been so blindly misguided, it should have supported and promoted this development with all means, not only because it would have naturally strengthened the ally but also because it might have provided the only opportunity to divert Italian interests away from the Adriatic and thus reduce friction with Austria-Hungary. Moreover, such a policy would have solidified the most natural opposition imaginable, namely that between Italy and France, thereby positively influencing the strengthening of the Triple Alliance.

It was unfortunate for Germany that at that time not only did the leadership of the Reich fail miserably, but also that public opinion, led by insane German nationalists and foreign policy fantasists, took a stand against Italy. This was especially regrettable because Austria interpreted Italy's actions in Tripolitania as something unfriendly. However, it was considered political wisdom among our national bourgeoisie to cover up any stupidity or malice of Viennese diplomacy, indeed if possible to adopt it oneself, in order to best demonstrate the internal harmony and steadfastness of this alliance to the world.

Now Austria-Hungary has been extinguished. However, Germany has less reason than ever to regret a development in Italy that must inevitably one day come at the expense of France. Because the more present-day Italy recalls its highest national tasks and accordingly transitions to a Roman-inspired spatial policy, the more it must come into conflict with its sharpest competitor in the Mediterranean Sea, France.

France will never tolerate Italy becoming a hegemon in the Mediterranean Sea. It will seek to prevent this either by its own strength alone or through a system of alliances. It will obstruct Italian development wherever possible and will not hesitate to resort to violence if necessary. The so-called kinship of the two Latin nations will not change this, as it is no closer than that between England and Germany.

Additionally, in the same proportion that France's own national strength diminishes, this state embarks on the exploitation of its black human reservoirs. Thus, a danger of unfathomable magnitude looms over Europe. The idea that French Negroes on the Rhine could poison the white blood as cultural guardians against Germany is so monstrous that only a few decades ago it would have been considered entirely impossible.

Certainly, through this contamination of blood, France itself will suffer the most severe damage, but only if the other European nations remain aware of the value of their white race. From a purely military perspective, France can indeed complement and effectively deploy its European formations, as demonstrated by the World War. Ultimately, this completely un-French black army even offers a certain protection against communist demonstrations, as blind obedience will be easier to maintain in all situations in an army not blood-related to the French people.

However, this development poses the greatest danger primarily to Italy. If the Italian people want to shape their future according to their own interests, they will one day have the black armies mobilized by France as their opponents. It can be in Italy's least interest to possess enmity towards Germany, which, even in the most favorable case, cannot contribute anything beneficial to shaping Italian life in the future. On the contrary, if any state can bury the enmity forever, it is Italy. Italy has no interest in further oppressing Germany if both states want to pursue their most natural future tasks.

Bismarck recognized this fortunate alignment. More than once, he emphasized the perfect parallelism of German and Italian interests. It was he who pointed out that Italy of the future will have to seek its development on the periphery of the Mediterranean Sea and also noted the harmony of Italian interests with those of Germany, emphasizing that only France can think of disrupting this Italian way of life, while Germany must welcome it from its own standpoint. He truly sees no necessary reason for estrangement or hostility between Italy and Germany in the future. If Bismarck had directed the fate of Germany before the World War instead of Bethmann Hollweg, this terrible enmity would never have occurred solely because of Austria.

Even more than with England, it is certain for Italy that Germany's continental expansion in Northern Europe cannot pose a threat and therefore cannot provide a reason for estrangement from Germany. Conversely, the most natural interests speak for Italy against any further increase in French hegemony in Europe.

Thus, primarily Italy would be a candidate for a federal relationship with Germany.

Since fascism has introduced a new state idea and with it a new will into the life of the Italian people, France's enmity has already become apparent. France seeks to strengthen itself for the possible confrontation with Italy through an entire system of alliances and to simultaneously encircle Italy's potential friends. The French goal is clear: to form a French system of states stretching from Paris through Warsaw, Prague, Vienna to Belgrade.

The attempt to include Austria in this system is by no means as hopeless as it may seem at first glance. Given the dominant character that the two-million city of Vienna exerts over the overall only six million people spanning Austria, the policy of this country will always be determined primarily by Vienna. The cosmopolitan nature of Vienna, which has become increasingly pronounced in the last decade, naturally makes an alliance with Paris far closer than one with Italy.

This is already ensured by the manipulation of public opinion guaranteed by the Viennese press. However, this activity threatens to be particularly effective since this press has succeeded, with the help of the South Tyrolean outcry, in inciting the completely instinctless bourgeois-national province against Italy. Thus, a danger of immeasurable magnitude looms. For a many-year consistently pursued press campaign can bring no people as easily as the German to the most incredible, indeed truly suicidal decisions.

However, if France succeeds in integrating Austria into the chain of its friendship, then Italy will one day be forced into a two-front war, or it will have to once again renounce the representation of the interests of the Italian people. In both cases, there is a danger for Germany that a potential ally will permanently withdraw from Germany for an unforeseeable period, thereby allowing France to increasingly become the master of Europe's destiny.

What this entails for Germany, there can be no illusion. Our bourgeois-national border politicians and patriotic protest organizations will then have their hands full constantly trying to erase the traces of mistreatment that they will endure from France thanks to their short-sighted policies.

Since the National Socialist movement has engaged in foreign policy considerations, I have attempted, taking into account all the motives mentioned, to educate it to be the bearer of a clear foreign policy goal. The accusation that this is primarily the task of the government is unjust, especially in a state whose official governments stem from the womb of parties that neither know nor desire a happy future for Germany. Since the responsible orchestrators of the November crime became capable of governing, the interests of the German nation are no longer represented, but only the interests of the parties mistreating it.

In general, one cannot expect people who view the fatherland and nation as mere means to an end, shamelessly sacrificed for their own benefits if necessary, to promote the necessities of German life. Indeed, the often visible self-preservation instinct of these people and parties alone speaks against any resurgence of the German nation, as the struggle for freedom for German honor would necessarily mobilize forces that should lead to the downfall and destruction of the current violators of German honor. There is no struggle for freedom without a general national resurgence.

However, a resurgence of national conscience and national honor is inconceivable without it becoming a judgment on those responsible for the previous dishonor. The selfish instinct for self-preservation will compel these degraded elements and their parties to sabotage all steps that could lead to a real resurrection of our people. And the apparent madness of some deeds of these Herostratuses of our people will, once the inner motives are appreciated, be revealed as a cunningly skilled, albeit infamous and pitiful act.

In such a time, when public life is shaped by parties of such a nature and is represented by individual people of the most inferior character, it is the duty of a national reform movement to also pursue its own foreign policy path, which must ultimately, according to all human foresight and reason, lead to the success and happiness of the fatherland. Thus, if this accusation of pursuing a policy that does not correspond to official foreign policy comes from Marxist-democratic-centralist circles, it can be dismissed with due contempt. If bourgeois-national and so-called patriotic circles raise it, then it is truly only the expression and symbol of a mentality of associative narrow-mindedness, which always only exercised itself in protests and which cannot seriously grasp the fact that another movement possesses the indestructible will to become a power and already now undertakes the necessary education of this power in anticipation of this fact.

Since the year 1920, I have endeavored with all means and persistence to accustom the National Socialist movement to the idea of an alliance between Germany, Italy, and England. This was very difficult, especially in the first years after the war, as the "God punish England" mentality initially robbed our people of any ability for clear and sober thinking in foreign policy matters and continued to hold them captive.

The situation for the young movement was infinitely difficult even with regard to Italy, especially since, under the leadership of the brilliant statesman Benito Mussolini, an unprecedented reorganization of the Italian people began, which drew the protest of all states directed by world Freemasons. For while until the year 1922 the manufacturers of public German opinion paid no attention whatsoever to the sufferings of the people separated from Germany by their crimes, they suddenly began to pay attention to South Tyrol. With all the means of cunning journalism and deceitful dialectics, the South Tyrolean problem was inflated into a matter of extraordinary significance, so that in the end, in Germany and Austria, Italy fell into disrepute unlike any other of the victorious powers. If the National Socialist movement was to honestly represent its foreign policy mission, driven by the conviction of its unconditional necessity, it could not shy away from taking up the fight against this system of lies and confusion. It had no ally to rely on, but had to be guided by the thought that it is better to forego popularity of a cheap kind than to act against a recognized truth, a present necessity, and the voice of one's own conscience. Even if it were to fail in doing so, it would still be more honorable than participating in a detected crime.

When I pointed out the possibility of future cooperation with Italy in 1920, it seemed that all the prerequisites for this were initially lacking. Italy was among the victorious powers and participated in the actual or perceived benefits of this situation. In 1919 and 1920, there seemed to be no prospect that the internal structure of the Entente would loosen in the foreseeable future. The mighty world coalition was still keen to show that it was a self-contained guarantor of victory and hence peace.

The difficulties that had already emerged during the drafting of the peace treaties were all the less apparent to the broader public, as a skillful management was always able to maintain the impression of complete uniformity outwardly. This joint appearance was both based on the public opinion achieved through the general similar war propaganda and on the still uncertain fear of the German giant. It was only slowly that the outside world gained insight into the magnitude of Germany's internal decay.

Another reason contributed to the almost insoluble cohesion of the victorious states: the hope of each individual not to be overlooked in the distribution of spoils in this way. Finally, it was also the fear that if indeed one state had withdrawn at that time, the fate of Germany would still have taken no other course; only the beneficiary of our collapse might then have been France alone. For in Paris, of course, there was no thought of bringing about a change in the attitude towards Germany adopted during the war. "Peace is for me the continuation of war." With this sentence, the old white-haired Clemenceau expressed the true intentions of the French people.

The apparent internal strength of the coalition of victors, inspired by France's unwavering goal of complete annihilation of Germany even after the fact, was countered by a complete lack of planning on the part of Germany. Alongside the pitiful villainy of those who, within their own country, falsely attributed blame for the war to Germany against all truth and their own knowledge, and shamelessly derived the justification for hostile extortions from it, stood a partly intimidated, partly uncertain national side, which believed that it could help the nation by reconstructing the past in the most painful way possible after the collapse had occurred. We lost the war due to a lack of national passion against our enemies.

The opinion among national circles was that, therefore, this disastrous lack must be replaced all the more, and that hatred against the former adversaries must be anchored in peace. It was noteworthy that from the beginning, this hatred was more concentrated against England and later Italy than against France. Against England, because thanks to Bethmann Hollweg's policy of appeasement, until the last hours, no one had believed in a war with England and thus perceived its entry as an extraordinary shameful breach of faith.

In the case of Italy, the hatred was even more understandable in the face of the political thoughtlessness of our German people. One had been so captivated by the mist and fog of the Triple Alliance from the official government circles that even Italy's non-intervention in favor of Austria-Hungary and Germany was perceived as a betrayal. In the later joining of the Italian people to our enemies, boundless perfidy was seen.

This accumulated hatred then erupted in the truly bourgeois-national thunderous words and battle cry: "God punish England." Since dear God is just as much with the stronger, more determined as he is with the wiser, he obviously rejected this punishment. Nevertheless, at least during the war, the incitement of our national passion with all means was not only permitted but also commanded.

It was only unfortunate that, despite the fact that passion was never excessively inflamed in us, we still lost sight of the real realities. There is no room for moral rectitude in politics, and therefore, even during the war, it was wrong, especially from Italy's entry into the world coalition, to draw no other consequences than those of flaring up anger and outrage. On the contrary, it would have been the duty to continually reassess the possibilities of the situation, in order to make the decisions that would have been necessary to save the threatened German nation.

For with Italy's entry into the Entente front, an extraordinary aggravation of the war situation was unavoidable, not only due to the increase in arms that the Entente received but much more due to the moral strengthening that must have lain in the emergence of such a power at the side of the world coalition, especially for France. At that time, the political leadership of the nation should have decided, no matter what the cost, to end the two- and three-front war. Germany was not responsible for the corrupt, inept Austrian state being preserved. The German soldier did not fight for the power politics of the Habsburg dynasty.

This may have been in the interest of our non-combatant cheerleaders, but not of the front shedding their blood. The suffering and hardships of the German musketeer were immeasurable as early as 1915. One could demand these sufferings for the future and preservation of our German people, but not for the salvation of Habsburg's grandiose delusions of power. It was an outrageous thought to let millions of German soldiers bleed in a hopeless war just to preserve the state of a dynasty whose very own dynastic interests had been anti-German for centuries.

This madness becomes fully understandable in its entirety when one considers that the best German blood had to be shed so that, in the best-case scenario, the Habsburgs would then have had the opportunity in peace to denationalize the German people. For this outrageous madness, not only was the most enormous blood sacrifice required on two fronts, but one was even obligated, time and again, to fill the gaps with German flesh and blood that the betrayal and corruption had torn into the ranks of the high ally. And yet, these sacrifices were made for a dynasty that was ready to abandon the all-sacrificing ally at the first opportunity.

And it did so later. Our bourgeois-national patriotic compatriots speak as little about the betrayal as they do about the ongoing betrayal of the allied Austrian war peoples, of Slavic nationality, who swung over to the enemy by regiments and brigades, and in the end, even participated in their own legions in the fight against those who had only been drawn into this terrible calamity by the actions of their state. Austria-Hungary would never have participated in a war that affected Germany on its own initiative.

It is due to the boundless ignorance of Austrian conditions prevailing in Germany that perhaps here or there, there was a genuine belief in having a mutually founded protection in the Triple Alliance. It would have been the worst disappointment for Germany if the World War had broken out due to a German cause. The fundamentally anti-German and anti-imperial Austrian state, with its Slavic majority and its Habsburg ruling house, would never have taken up arms to protect and assist Germany against a whole other world, as Germany unfortunately did. In fact, Germany had only one obligation to fulfill towards Austria-Hungary, namely: to save the Germanic nature of this state by all means and to eliminate the degenerate, most guilt-laden dynasty that the German people had ever had to endure.

Italy's entry into the World War should have been the occasion for Germany to fundamentally reconsider its position towards Austria-Hungary. It is not a political act or even the result of political leadership of prudence and ability to find no other response in such a case than bitter anger and impotent fury. Such a thing is usually harmful in private life, but in politics, it is worse than a crime. It is stupidity.

And even if this attempt to change the previous German attitude had not led to success, it would have at least acquitted the political leadership of the nation of the guilt of not having tried. In any case, Germany had to try to bring an end to the two-front war after Italy's entry into the World War. Then, a separate peace with Russia had to be sought, not only on the basis of renouncing any exploitation of the successes achieved in the East by German weapons so far but even, if necessary, at the cost of sacrificing Austria-Hungary. Only the complete detachment of German politics from the task of saving the Austrian state and its exclusive concentration on the task of helping the German people could still offer a prospect of victory according to human understanding.

Moreover, in the event of the disintegration of Austria-Hungary, the annexation of 9 million German Austrians to the Reich would have been a more valuable success in the eyes of history and for the future of our people than the questionable gain of a few French coal or iron mines. However, it must be emphasized time and again that the task of even a bourgeois-national

German foreign policy would not have been the preservation of the Habsburg state, but exclusively the salvation of the German nation, including the 9 million Germans in Austria. And nothing else, absolutely nothing else.

The reaction of the German imperial leadership to the new situation created by Italy's entry into the World War was, as is well known, different. They attempted, even more so, to save the Austrian state from the deserting Slavic brethren by bringing German blood into even greater use and invoking the heavens' vengeance upon the faithless former allies at home. However, in order to bar any possibility of ending the two-front war, they were persuaded by the cunning Viennese diplomacy to establish the Polish state. Thus, any hope of reaching an understanding with Russia, which would naturally have affected Austria-Hungary's interests, was cleverly thwarted by the Habsburgs. The German soldiers from Bavaria and Pomerania, Westphalia, Thuringia, and East Prussia, from Brandenburg, Saxony, and the Rhine, thus had the high honor of giving their lives in terrible, bloodiest battles in world history, not for the salvation of the German nation, but for the establishment of a Polish state, to which, in the event of a favorable world war outcome, the Habsburgs would have given a representative, and which would have been an eternal enemy of Germany.

Bourgeois-national state policy. But if this reaction to the Italian move in wartime was already unforgivable madness, then the preservation of the emotional reaction to the Italian move after the war was an even greater, capital stupidity.

Certainly, Italy was still part of the coalition of the victorious powers after the war and thus on the side of France. But it was only natural, since Italy had not entered the war out of pro-French sentiments. The driving force that led the Italian people to do so was solely the hatred of Austria and the visible possibility of benefiting their own Italian interests.

This was the reason for Italy's actions and not some fantastic sentiment for France. That Italy drew far-reaching consequences after the collapse of its hated century-old adversary can be felt with deepest pain as a German, but it must not cloud the senses of sound reason. Fate had turned. Once Austria had over 800,000 Italians under its rule, and now 200,000 Austrians fell under the rule of Italy. That these 200,000 of German nationality concern us is the cause of our pain.

With the resolution of the eternal latent Austrian-Italian conflict, the future goals of neither a national nor ethnocentric Italian policy are fulfilled. On the contrary, the tremendous increase in the self-awareness and power of the Italian people through the war and especially through Fascism will only enhance its strength in pursuing greater objectives. Thus, the natural conflicting interests between Italy and France will increasingly come to the forefront.

This could already be expected and hoped for in the years 1920. Indeed, even then, the very first signs of internal disharmony between the two states were apparent. While the South Slavic instincts were assured of further diminishment of Austrian-Germanism and garnered undivided sympathy from France, the Italian stance, especially during the liberation of Carinthia from the Slavs, was at least very benevolent towards the German cause.

This internal shift towards Germany was also evident in the attitude of Italian commissions in Germany itself, most notably during the conflicts in Upper Silesia. In any case, one could already discern the beginning of a, albeit initially slight, internal alienation between the two Latin nations. According to all human logic, reason, and based on all previous experiences in history, this alienation must deepen over time and must one day culminate in open conflict. Italy will, whether it wants to or not, have to fight against France for the existence and future of its state just as Germany itself.

It is not necessary for France to always be at the forefront of the actions. However, it will pull the strings of those whom it has cunningly brought into financial and military dependence or with whom it appears connected through parallel interests. The Italian-French confrontation could finally begin at the Balkans and perhaps end in the Lombardian plains.

Given this compelling probability of Italy's later enmity with France, it seemed already in 1920 that this state, above all, was likely to become a future federal state for Germany. This probability turned into certainty with the victory of Fascism, which eliminated the weak Italian government, ultimately subject to international influences, and replaced it with a regime that had exclusively adopted the representation of Italian interests as its motto. A weak Italian-democratic-bourgeois government might have maintained an artificial relationship with France, disregarding Italy's real future tasks, but a national-conscious and responsible Italian regime never could. On the day when the fasces became the Italian national emblem, the struggle of the Third Rome for the future of the Italian people received its historical declaration. Thus, one of the two Latin nations will have to yield the place at the Mediterranean Sea, while the other will receive dominance as the prize of this struggle.

As a nationally conscious and rational-thinking German, I have the firm hope and strongest desire that this may be Italy and not France. Thus, my behavior towards Italy is motivated by forward-looking reasons and not by barren memories of the war.

The standpoint "Here war declarations are accepted" was a good sign of the victorious confidence of the old army when displayed on troop transports. However, as a political creed, it is sheer folly. Even more absurd is the notion that Germany should not consider any former adversaries of the World War as potential allies and instead, engage in hostility towards them.

When Marxists, Democrats, and centrists adopt such an idea as the guiding principle of their political actions, it is evident because this corrupt coalition never desires the resurgence of the German nation. However, when national bourgeois and patriotic circles embrace such thoughts, then everything loses its meaning. For, name any power in Europe that could be considered as an ally for Germany, which has not enriched itself territorially at the expense of ours or our former allies during the war.

From this standpoint, France is excluded from the outset because it annexed Alsace-Lorraine and aims to annex the Rhineland. Belgium is excluded because it possesses Eupen and Malmedy. England, although it does not possess our colonies, administers them, which in the course of international affairs means domination. Denmark is excluded because it took Northern Schleswig, Poland because it has Western Prussia, Upper Silesia, and parts of East Prussia, the Czechoslovakia because it oppresses nearly 4 million Germans, Romania because it annexed over 1 million Germans, Yugoslavia because it possesses nearly 600,000 Germans, and Italy because it currently owns South Tyrol.

Thus, the possibilities for alliances in Europe are completely impossible for our national bourgeois and patriotic circles. But they do not need them, as they will either stifle or collapse the resistance of the rest of the world through the flood of their protests and the roar of their hurrahs. And then, without any allies, even without any weapons, relying only on the steadfastness of their verbal protests, they will reclaim the annexed territories, punish England retroactively through divine retribution, chastise Italy, and subject it to the deserved contempt of the entire world – unless they have been hung from the lampposts by their current political allies, the Bolshevik and Marxist Jews, by then.

It is remarkable that our national circles of bourgeois and patriotic origin do not realize that the strongest proof of the fallacy of their foreign policy stance lies in the approval of the Marxists, Democrats, centrists, and particularly in the approval of the Jews. But one must be familiar with our German civic spirit to immediately understand why this is so. They are all infinitely happy to have found at least one matter in which the presumed unity of the German people appears to be restored.

Even if it involves sheer folly, it is still infinitely gratifying for a courageous bourgeois and patriotic politician to be able to speak in nationalistic tones without immediately receiving a slap from the nearest communist. Yet, the reason they are spared is only because their political viewpoint, whether national or Jewish-Marxist, is as barren as it is valuable. It is outrageous to witness the extent to which the corruption of lies and cowardice has taken hold among us.

When in 1920 I shifted the movement's foreign policy focus towards Italy, I initially encountered complete incomprehension from both the national circles and what are known as the patriotic circles. For these people, it was simply incomprehensible how one could conceive a political idea contrary to the general obligation of constant protests, which practically meant an internal liquidation of one of the enmities of the World War. In general, the national circles failed to understand why I did not want to place the main emphasis of national activity on protests, which are shouted into the blue sky in front of the Munich Feldherrnhalle or somewhere else, sometimes against Paris, then against London, or even against Rome, rather than focusing on eliminating those responsible for the collapse within Germany itself.

Following the Paris Dictate, there was also a fervent protest rally against Paris in Munich, which probably did not concern Mr. Clemenceau much but prompted me to sharply outline the national socialist stance opposed to this protest frenzy. France had only done what any German could and should have known. If I were French myself, I would have naturally stood behind Clemenceau.

Continuously barking at a powerful opponent from afar is as undignified as it is foolish. In contrast, the national opposition of these patriotic circles should have shown their teeth to those responsible and guilty for the terrible catastrophe of our collapse in Berlin. However, it was more pleasant to curse Paris, although there was no possibility of realizing those curses given the actual circumstances, than to take action against Berlin.

This especially applied to the representatives of Bavarian state policy, whose past successes already revealed their remarkable ingenuity. Indeed, the men who constantly claimed to want to preserve Bavaria's sovereign rights, while also considering the preservation of the right to engage in foreign policy, would have been obligated to positively advocate for a possible foreign policy in such a way that Bavaria would inevitably lead a truly national opposition in Germany, based on significant considerations. Given the complete disarray of imperial politics or the intended negation of all real possibilities for success, Bavaria, in particular, should have risen to become the spokesperson for a foreign policy that, by human foresight, would have eventually brought an end to Germany's appalling isolation.

Yet, even there, in these circles, my advocated foreign policy stance of alignment with Italy was met with complete thoughtless stupidity. Instead of rising in such a magnanimous way to become the spokesperson and guardian of the highest national German interests, they preferred to occasionally wink at Paris and, while raising their eyes to the sky, profess their loyalty to the Reich on one hand but on the other hand, expressed their resolve to save Bavaria by allowing the North to be burned down by Bolshevism. Yes, indeed, these are truly extraordinary intellectual phenomena entrusted with representing their sovereign rights by the Bavarian state.

Given such a general mentality, no one should be surprised that my foreign policy stance, if not directly rejected, was at least completely incomprehensible from the very beginning. Frankly speaking, I did not expect anything else at the time. I still counted on the prevailing war psychosis and only endeavored to instill sober foreign policy thinking within my own movement.

At that time, I did not have to endure any open attacks because of my Italy policy. On the one hand, this was probably because they were considered completely harmless at the moment, and on the other hand, Italy itself also had a government susceptible to international influences. Moreover, perhaps in the background, there was even hope that Italy might succumb to the Bolshevik plague, and then, at least for our leftist circles, it would have been highly welcome as an ally in itself.

Furthermore, at that time, it was not easy for the left to take a stand against the dismantling of wartime enmity, as they constantly endeavored to eradicate the ugly, degrading, and unjustified feeling of war hatred towards Germany. It would have been difficult for them to criticize me from within these circles for a foreign policy stance that, as a prerequisite for its realization, required at least the dismantling of war hatred between Germany and Italy.

I must emphasize once again that perhaps the main reason why I encountered so little positive resistance from my opponents lay in the perceived harmlessness, impracticability, and thus, the lack of danger of my actions. This situation changed almost as if by magic when Mussolini began the March on Rome. From that moment on, as if on cue, the drumbeat of poisoning and slander through the entire Jewish press against Italy commenced. And only after the year 1922 was the South Tyrolean question raised and, whether the South Tyroleans liked it or not, made the focal point of German-Italian relations.

It did not take long before even Marxism became a representative of a national opposition, and one could now witness the unique spectacle of Jews and German nationalists, Social Democrats and patriotic associations, Communists and the national bourgeoisie, arm in arm, mentally crossing the Brenner Pass to carry out, in massive battles albeit without bloodshed, the reconquest of this territory. The fact that even those Bavarian representatives of state sovereignty who were more ur-Bavarian showed a lively interest in the fight for the Andreas Hofer Land, despite their intellectual forebears having handed over the good Andreas Hofer to the French about 100 years ago and then had him executed, lent this bold national front a very special allure.

Now, since the machinations of the Jewish press mob and their trailing national bourgeois and patriotic fools have truly succeeded in elevating the South Tyrolean problem to the magnitude of a life-or-death issue for the German nation, I feel compelled to address it in detail.

As emphasized earlier, the old Austrian state had just over 850,000 Italians within its borders. However, the nationalities ratio determined by the Austrian censuses was not entirely accurate. This was because they counted not the nationality of the individual but only their stated vernacular language.

It's obvious that this method couldn't provide a completely clear picture, but it was also a weakness of the national bourgeoisie to prefer being deceived about the real situation. If one doesn't learn about something or at least doesn't openly talk about it, then it doesn't exist. The Italians, or rather, people with Italian vernacular language based on such a method, lived to a very large extent in Tyrol. According to the results of the 1910 census, Tyrol had ... inhabitants, of which ... percent claimed Italian as their vernacular language, while the rest were German or, in part, Ladin. Consequently, there were around ... Italians in the Archduchy of Tyrol.

Since this entire number falls within the territory currently occupied by Italians, the ratio of Germans to Italians in the entire section of Tyrol occupied by Italy is that of ... Germans to ... Italians. It's necessary to establish this because many people in Germany, thanks to the mendacity of our press, have no idea that in the area understood by the term South Tyrol, there are 2/3 Italians and 1/3 Germans. Therefore, anyone who seriously advocates for the reconquest of South Tyrol would only bring about a change in the situation to the extent that instead of 200,000 Germans under Italian rule, there would be 400,000 Italians under German rule.

However, German culture in South Tyrol is predominantly concentrated in the northern part, while Italian culture inhabits the southern part.

Therefore, if someone were to seek a nationally just solution, they would first have to completely exclude the term South Tyrol from the general discussion. Because one cannot morally condemn Italians for taking a territory where, alongside 400,000 Italians, there are also 200,000 Germans, if one intends, conversely, to reclaim that same territory for Germany, thereby committing an even greater injustice from a purely moral standpoint than Italy did. Thus, the call for the reconquest of South Tyrol will have the same moral flaws as those currently found in Italian rule over South Tyrol.

Consequently, this call also loses its moral justification. Other perspectives could then be put forward that would speak for the reconquest of all of South Tyrol. Thus, from generally morally justified sentiments, one could at most advocate for the reconquest of that part which is predominantly inhabited by Germans. This is a spatially limited area of ... square kilometers. Yet even there, around 190,000 Germans encounter 64,000 Italians and Ladin speakers, and 24,000 other foreigners, so that the entirely German area actually comprises scarcely 160,000 Germans.

There are hardly any current borders in Europe that do not, similar to in South Tyrol, cut off Germans from the motherland. Indeed, alone in Europe, not less than ... million Germans are separated from the Reich. Of these, ... million live under outright foreign rule, and only ... million, namely in German-Austria and Switzerland, live under circumstances that are at least for the moment not threatening to their nationality. Here, in a whole series of cases, it concerns numerically different complexes of our people compared to South Tyrol.

As terrible as this fact is for our people, those who are now raising a clamor about South Tyrol are guilty of it. However, even with the adoption of a purely bourgeois border policy, the fate of the entire remaining Reich cannot simply be made dependent on the interests of these lost territories or even on the wishes of one of them.

Because something must first be categorically rejected: There is no sacred German people in South Tyrol, as the patriotic associations chatter. Rather, everything that must be counted as part of the German ethnic group should be equally sacred to the German people. It is not permissible to esteem a South Tyrolean higher than a Silesian, East Prussian, or West Prussian who is oppressed under Polish rule. It is also not acceptable to consider a German in Czechoslovakia as more valuable than a German in the Saar region or in Alsace-Lorraine. Sorting the German heritage of the detached territories according to special values is only permissible if it stems from an analytical examination of their respective decisive and dominant racial values. However, the protest union against Italy applies this yardstick least of all. It would also undoubtedly not assign a higher value factor to the Tyrolean in today's ceded territories than, for example, to an East or West Prussian.

In essence, the foreign policy task of the German people cannot be determined by the interests of one of the parts splintered from the Reich. Because in reality, serving these interests in this way is not achieved, since practical assistance presupposes the regained power of the motherland. Consequently, the only consideration that comes into question for taking a foreign policy stance must be that which most quickly and effectively achieves the restoration of the independence and freedom of the nationally consolidated remnants of the nation.

In other words, even if German foreign policy had no other goal than the rescue of the sacred people in South Tyrol, meaning the 190,000 Germans who are truly relevant in this context, the prerequisite for this would be the attainment of political independence and military means by Germany. Because it is quite clear that the Austrian protest state will not wrest South Tyrol from the Italians. Equally clear, however, must be that even if German foreign policy had no other goal than the actual liberation of South Tyrol, its actions would still have to be determined by considerations and moments that provide the conditions for regaining political and military means.

Therefore, South Tyrol should not be brought to the forefront of foreign policy considerations, but rather should be governed and guided by those thoughts that allow for the breaking of the current world coalition against Germany. For indeed, South Tyrol would not be returned to the German people by Germany itself by merely reciting a litany of protests and indignations, but by the use of the sword. So even if Germany possessed this goal itself, it would still need to continuously seek an ally who would assist in gaining German power.

Now, one might say that France could be considered for this case.

However, as a National Socialist, I vehemently oppose this. It may be that France would agree to let Germany march with it against Italy as an auxiliary force, yes, it may even be that, as recognition of our blood sacrifices and as a meager salve for our wounds, it would grant us South Tyrol.

However, what would such a victory mean for Germany? Could our people then live just because they possess 200,000 more South Tyroleans? Or does one not believe that France, once it had defeated its Latin competitor at the Mediterranean with German military aid, would turn against Germany once again? In any case, it would surely pursue its old political goal of the dissolution of Germany even more vigorously?

No, if Germany has any choice between France and Italy, then, according to all human reason, only Italy can be considered for Germany. Because a victory with France over Italy brings us South Tyrol and, furthermore, a stronger France as a subsequent enemy. A victory for Germany over France with Italy's help brings us Alsace-Lorraine at least, and at most, the freedom to implement a truly generous spatial policy. And only from this can Germany live in the future, not from South Tyrol.

However, it is simply not feasible to single out one of the entirely detached territories, the least vital one, and jeopardize the entire interests of a 70-million-strong nation, or even to forsake its future, just so that the unfortunate German fantastic hurrah-patriotism can receive momentary satisfaction. And all this for the sake of a pure phantom, as in reality, South Tyrol would be no better off than it is now.

The National Socialist movement must educate the German people to be willing to sacrifice blood for the shaping of their lives. However, our people must also be educated to ensure that such a sacrifice of blood never again occurs for phantoms in the future. Our protest patriots and patriotic associations should have the honesty to say how they envision the reconquest of South Tyrol other than through armed force.

They should have the honesty to admit whether they truly believe that Italy, one day, will simply relinquish South Tyrol due to rhetoric and protests, or whether they are convinced that a state with some existing national consciousness will only sacrifice a territory it fought for over four years under the duress of a military decision. They should stop claiming that we, or I, have renounced South Tyrol. These infamous liars know very well that at least regarding myself, during the time when the fate of South Tyrol was being decided, I fought at the front, something many of today's association protesters failed to do.

However, during that same time, the forces with which our patriotic associations and national bourgeoisie now engage in common foreign policy and incite against Italy sabotaged victory by all means. The International Marxism, democracy, and the center did not miss any opportunity in peacetime to weaken and paralyze the military strength of our people. They ultimately organized a revolution during the war that led to the collapse of the German homeland and thus the German army.

Through the activities of these individuals and the cursed weakness and impotence of our current bourgeois protesters, South Tyrol has been lost to the German people. It is a pathetic forgery of these so-called national patriots to speak today of renunciation of South Tyrol. No, my esteemed gentlemen, do not cowardly evade the right word. Do not be afraid to admit that today it could only be about the conquest of South Tyrol.

For the renunciation, my gentlemen national association protesters, was legally executed in all forms by your current high allies, the Marxist traitors of yesteryear. And the only ones who had the courage to openly oppose this crime were not you, my gentlemen national association members and bourgeois politicians, but the small National Socialist movement, and primarily myself. Yes, my gentlemen, when nobody in Germany had any idea of your existence due to your silence, you were hiding in your mouse holes. At that time, in 1919 and 1920, I stood against the shame of signing the peace treaties. And not in secret, behind closed doors, but publicly.

But at that time, you were still so cowardly that you didn't even dare to come to our meetings, fearing to be beaten by your current external political allies, the Marxist street thugs. The men who signed the Treaty of St. Germain were no more National Socialists than those who signed the Treaty of Versailles. They were members of parties who, by signing these treaties, only crowned their decades-long treason.

Whoever wants to change the fate of South Tyrol today cannot renounce anymore because renunciation has already been executed in all forms by today's protesters, but they could only reconquer it.

Against this, however, I vehemently oppose and declare the most extreme resistance to this endeavor, and I will fight with utmost fanaticism against the men who attempt to involve our people in this equally bloody and insane adventure. I did not experience the war from the comfort of a tavern. Nor was I one of those who had anything to command or to order in this war. I was just an ordinary soldier who was commanded for 4 1/2 years, yet still fulfilled his duty honestly and faithfully.

However, I was fortunate enough to experience the war as it truly is and not as one would like to see it. Until the very last hour of this war, even as a simple soldier who only knew its darker side, I supported the war because I believed that only in victory could the salvation of our people lie. But now, as there is a peace that others have violated, I resist vehemently against a war that would not benefit the German people but only those who previously shamelessly sold the blood sacrifices of our people for their own interests.

I am convinced that I will not lack determination when the time comes to bear responsibility for a blood sacrifice of the German people if necessary. But I resist dragging even a single German onto a battlefield from whose blood only fools or criminals nourish their plans. Anyone who contemplates the unimaginable horrors and the terrible misery of a modern war, who considers the boundless strain on the nerves of a nation, must recoil at the thought that such a sacrifice could be demanded for a success that, in the best case, could never match this sacrifice.

And I also know that if today the people of South Tyrol, as far as they think German, were to be assembled on a single front, and before the eyes of these spectators appeared the 100,000 and hundreds of thousands of dead that the fight for them would impose on our people, then 300,000 hands would rise defensively to the sky, and the foreign policy of the National Socialists would be justified. But the dreadful thing about all of this is that these appalling possibilities are being played with without even considering wanting to help the South Tyroleans. As the fight for South Tyrol is now led by those who once abandoned all of Germany to ruin, South Tyrol is also just a means to an end for them, which they apply with ice-cold ruthlessness to satisfy their infamous, in the highest sense of the word, anti-German instincts.

It is hatred against today's national-conscious Italy, and above all, it is hatred against the new state idea of this country and, highest of all, it is hatred against the outstanding Italian statesman that prompts them to incite the German public with the help of South Tyrol. For how indifferent are these elements to the German people in reality. While they lament the fate of South Tyrol with crocodile tears, they are leading all of Germany towards a fate worse than that of the severed territories.

While they protest against Italy in the name of national culture, they pollute the culture of the German nation internally, destroy our entire cultural sensibility, poison the instincts of our people, and even destroy the achievements of past times. Does a time have a moral right to act in the name of culture against present-day Italy or to protect German culture from being pushed down to the level of pigs by our entire theater, literature, and visual arts? Concern for the German culture of the South Tyroleans is shown by the gentlemen of the Bavarian People's Party, the German Nationals, and even the Marxist cultural desecrators, but they allow the culture of the homeland to be insulted by the most miserable works undisturbed, deliver the German stages to the racial shame of a Johnny Plays On and hypocritically lament the suppression of German cultural life in South Tyrol, while they themselves mercilessly persecute those at home who wanted to protect German culture from deliberate and intended destruction. Here, the Bavarian People's Party incites state power against those who protest against the infamous desecration of the culture of our people. What do they do, these concerned guardians of German culture, in South Tyrol, in Germany itself, to protect German culture?

They have allowed the theater to sink to the level of a brothel, to a place of demonstrated racial shame, let the cinema mock decency and morality, destroy all the foundations of our national life; they stand by during the cubist and dadaist infatuation of our visual arts, they themselves protect the manufacturers of this common deceit or madness; they let German literature sink into mud and filth and deliver the entire intellectual life of our people to the international Jew. And the same wretched bunch then have the audacity to advocate for German culture in South Tyrol, but naturally, their goal is only the incitement of two cultured peoples, making it easier in the end to press them to the level of their own cultureless wretchedness.

But it's the same in everything. They lament the persecution of Germans in South Tyrol, yet these are the same people who in Germany vehemently oppose anyone who understands something different by nationalism than exposing his people defenseless to syphilization by Jews and Negroes. The same people who cry out for the freedom of conscience of Germans in South Tyrol suppress it most despicably in Germany itself.

Never before has the freedom of expression of one's national sentiments in Germany been so stifled as under the rule of this deceitful party riffraff, which presumes to champion the rights of conscience and national freedoms especially in South Tyrol. They bemoan every injustice done to a German in South Tyrol, but remain silent about the murders committed by these Marxist street riffraff against the national element in Germany month after month, and with them, this whole clean national bourgeoisie including the patriotic protesters. In just one year, that is, only five months of this year have passed, nine people have been killed and over 600 wounded solely from the ranks of the National Socialist movement, some under bestial circumstances.

Yet this entire deceitful brood remains silent. But how they would howl if only a single such act were committed by fascism against the Germanic people in South Tyrol. They would call the whole world to rebellion if even a single German in South Tyrol were slaughtered by fascists under similar circumstances to those the Marxist gang of murderers applies in Germany, without this arousing the outrage of this clean phalanx to save the German people. And yet these same people who solemnly protest against the official persecution of Germans in South Tyrol have persecuted the inconvenient Germans in the Reich itself. How here, from the U-boat heroes to the saviors of Upper Silesia, have the men who first put their blood for Germany been dragged in chains before courts and finally sentenced to prison terms, all because they have risked their lives for the fatherland a hundred and a hundred times over, while this wretched protest mob had disappeared somewhere without a trace.

They may add up the prison sentences imposed in Germany for actions that would have been rewarded with the highest distinctions in a nation conscious of its identity. When Italy today arrests a German in South Tyrol, the entire German national and Marxist press immediately clamors. But that in Germany one can be imprisoned for months on mere denunciation, that house searches, violation of the secrecy of correspondence, wiretapping, all unconstitutional violations of personal freedom guaranteed by civil rights in this country, are commonplace, they completely overlook.

And our so-called national parties may not claim that this is only possible in Marxist Prussia. Firstly, they are now arm in arm with these same Marxists in foreign policy, and secondly, these same national parties have had the same share in suppressing a truly self-confident nationalism. In national Bavaria, the terminally ill Dietrich Eckart, despite medical certificates attesting to no trace of any guilt other than that of his incorruptible national sentiment, was thrown into so-called protective custody and kept there until he finally collapsed and died two days after his release.

Yet he was Bavaria's greatest poet, of course, he was a national German and committed no offense like "Jonny Plays On," and therefore he did not exist for these champions of national culture. Just as these national patriots once killed him, they now silence his works, because he was only a German and a good Bavarian, not an internationally Jewish Germany-defiler. In that case, he would have been sacred to this league of patriots, but since he was just a German, they acted in accordance with their national-bourgeois sentiment with the openly expressed call in the Munich Police Directorate: National swine, perish.

But these are the same German-conscious elements who mobilize the world's outrage when a German is foolishly arrested in Italy. When a few Germans were expelled from South Tyrol, the same people once again called the entire German people to bright outrage, but they forget to add that in Germany itself, Germans were most incited. National Bavaria under a bourgeois national government has expelled dozens of Germans because they politically did not fit the corrupt bourgeois stratum due to their uncompromising nationalism.

Then one suddenly no longer knew the tribal fraternity with the Germans from Austria, but only the foreigner. But the expulsion of so-called foreign

Germans did not stop there. No, the same bourgeois-national hypocrites who hurl flaming protests against Italy for expelling a German from South Tyrol and deporting him to another province have expelled dozens of Germans with German citizenship from Bavaria.

Yes, these bourgeois-national hypocrites, who now rage in indignation against Italy, while they themselves have loaded shame upon shame on their own people. They lament the denationalization in Italy while denationalizing the German people in their own homeland. They fight against anyone who opposes the blood poisoning of our people, indeed they persecute every German who opposes, in the most impudent and ruthless manner, the denationalization, negrification, and Judaization of our people staged and protected by them in the big cities, and try to throw them into prison by falsely alleging a threat to religious institutions.

When an Italian ex-soldier damaged the Empress Elizabeth monument in Merano, they raised a wild outcry and could not calm down, although an Italian court had punished the perpetrator with 2 months' imprisonment. But they are not interested in the fact that in Germany itself, the monuments and memories of the past greatness of our people are continuously besmirched. The fact that in France almost all monuments reminding of Germany in Alsace-Lorraine have been destroyed does not concern them, nor does it bother them that the Poles systematically destroy everything that reminds them of the German name, or that just in recent months in Bromberg the Bismarck tower was officially blown up.

All this leaves them indifferent, these fighters for the national honor of our people. But woe betide if something like this were to happen in South Tyrol. For suddenly that has become sacred ground to them. But the fatherland itself, the homeland, can go to hell.

Certainly, there have been more than a few unwise actions on the Italian side in South Tyrol, and the attempt to systematically denationalize the German element is just as unwise as it is questionable in its outcome. However, the right to protest against this does not belong to those who are partly responsible for it and who, on the other hand, actually do not know the national honor of their people, but rather this right belongs to those who have truly fought for German interests and German honor. This was exclusively the National Socialist movement in Germany.

The entire internal hypocrisy of the agitation against Italy becomes visible when comparing the actions of the Italians with the actions committed by the French, Poles, Belgians, Czechs, Romanians, and South Slavs against the German people. The fact that France has expelled over a quarter of a million Germans from Alsace-Lorraine, more people than the entire population of South Tyrol, is of no concern to them. And the fact that the French are now trying to eradicate every trace of Germanness in Alsace-Lorraine does not prevent them from fraternizing with France, even if continual slaps in the face are Paris's response.

The fact that the Belgians persecute the German element with unparalleled fanaticism, that the Poles have slaughtered over 17,000 Germans, some under downright bestial circumstances, is not a cause for concern, nor is the fact that they have finally expelled tens of thousands from their homes and driven them across the border with barely a shirt on their backs. These are all things that our bourgeois and patriotic protest hypocrites cannot seem to get worked up about. Indeed, anyone who wants to get to know the true sentiments of this pack need only remember how they treated the refugees back then.

Their hearts did not bleed for them back then, any more than they do today, when tens of thousands of unhappily displaced people found themselves back in their beloved homeland, some in formal concentration camps, and were now being deported from place to place like gypsies. I still remember the time when the first refugees from the Ruhr came to Germany and were then deported from police department to police department as if they were hardened criminals. No, their hearts did not bleed for them, these representatives and defenders of the national German spirit in South Tyrol.

But if even a single German is expelled from South Tyrol by the Italians or if any other injustice is inflicted, then they tremble with righteous indignation and outrage over this single cultural disgrace and this greatest barbarity that the world has ever seen. How they then say: Never before has Germanhood been suppressed with such appalling and tyrannical methods as in these lands. Yes, but with one exception, namely in Germany itself, through your own tyranny.

Certainly, South Tyrol, or rather the Germanic heritage in South Tyrol, must be preserved for the German people. However, in Germany itself, they annually murder more than twice as many people through their infamous policy of dishonorable internationalism, general corruption, and submission to international financial masters, as the entire population of Germans in South Tyrol counts. They remain silent about the 17,000-22,000 people driven to suicide on average in recent years due to their disastrous policies, even though this number alone would be more than the entire population of Germans in South Tyrol in 10 years, including children.

They condone emigration, and increasing emigration quotas, according to this national bourgeoisie represented by Mr. Stresemann, are considered a great foreign policy success, yet this means that Germany loses more people every four years than South Tyrol has inhabitants of German nationality. However, they almost double the number of people killed each year through abortion and birth control as the Germanic population in South Tyrol amounts to in total. And this pack then claims the moral right to speak for the interests of Germanic people abroad.

Or this official national Germany laments the de-Germanization of our language in South Tyrol, but in Germany itself, they officially de-Germanize German names in Czechoslovakia, Alsace-Lorraine, and elsewhere. Official travel guides are published in which even our German city names in Germany are Germanized for the Czechs' sake. That's all fine, but the Italians changing the holy name Brenner to Brennero is cause for the most vehement resistance. And one must have seen this bourgeois patriot begin to glow with holy national indignation, knowing full well that it's all just a farce.

Feigning national passion suits our passionless, corrupt bourgeoisie just as well as when an old hag pretends to be in love. It's all artificial acting, and it's worst when such excitement originates from Austria. The black-yellow legitimist element, which used to be completely indifferent to Germanism in Tyrol, now joins in holy national outrage. Such a thing electrifies all bourgeois associations, especially when they hear that even the Jews are participating.

That means they themselves only protest because they know that this time, for once, they can loudly proclaim their national sentiment without being fired into a corner by the press Jews. On the contrary: It's quite nice for an upright bourgeois national man to call for national struggle and even be praised by ItzigVeitel Abrahamsohn. Yes, even more. The Jewish gazettes join in, thus creating the first real bourgeois national German unity front from Krotoschin to Vienna to Innsbruck. And our politically foolish German people fall for this whole theater just as much as German diplomacy and our German people were once ensnared and abused by the Habsburgs.

Germany has once allowed its foreign policy to be determined exclusively by Austrian interests. The punishment for this was terrible. Woe betide if young German nationalism lets its future policy be determined by the theatrical prattlers of the decaying bourgeois element or even by Marxist German enemies. And woe betide if, once again, in complete ignorance of the truly driving forces of the Austrian state in Vienna, it derives its directives from there. It will be the task of the National Socialist movement to put an end to this actor's outcry and to choose sober reason as the ruler of future German foreign policy.

However, Italy also bears some responsibility for this whole development. I would consider it foolish and politically childish to blame the Italian state for shifting the border to the Brenner in the aftermath of the Austrian collapse. The motives that governed them were no baser than the motives that determined bourgeois annexationist policies, including Mr. Stresemann and Mr. Erzberger, to support the German border up to the Belgian Maas fortresses. Throughout history, a responsible and thinking state government will strive to find strategically natural and secure borders. Certainly, Italy did not annex South Tyrol to gain possession of a few hundred thousand Germans; it would have preferred if only Italians lived in this area instead of Germans. Indeed, it was never primarily strategic considerations that prompted them to place the border beyond the Brenner.

However, no state would have acted differently in a similar situation. It is therefore pointless to make accusations about this border arrangement, as ultimately every state determines its natural borders according to its own interests, not others'. As much as the possession of the Brenner may serve military interests and strategic purposes, it is inconsequential whether 200,000 Germans live within this strategically established and secured border or not when the national population itself comprises 42 million people and a militarily effective opponent is not a concern at this border.

It would have been wiser to spare these 200,000 Germans any coercion rather than forcibly trying to instill a sentiment in them, which, as experience shows, tends to be worthless as a result of such coercion. One cannot eradicate a nationality in 20 or 30 years, no matter what methods are used or whether one wants to or not. On the Italian side, one might respond with a certain semblance of justification that this was not initially intended, but rather developed as a consequence of the provocative attempt at continuous interference in Italian internal affairs by external Austrian or German forces and the resulting repercussions among the South Tyroleans themselves.

This is correct because indeed, initially, the Italians treated the Germanic population in South Tyrol very decently and loyally. However, when fascism rose to prominence in Italy, the agitation against Italy began in Germany and Austria for principled reasons, leading to increasing mutual irritation, which eventually had to lead to consequences in South Tyrol as we see them today. Unfortunate in this regard was primarily the action of the Andreas Hofer Bund, which instead of advising prudence to the Germans in South Tyrol and making it clear to them that their mission was to build a bridge between Germany and Italy, raised hopes among the South Tyroleans that were beyond any feasibility but had to lead to incitement and thus to ill-considered steps.

It is primarily due to this association that the situation was exacerbated. Having had ample opportunity to get to know essential members of this association as individuals, I am amazed at the irresponsibility with which a union of such meager truly active forces still manages to cause disastrous harm. Because when I consider various of these leading figures and think especially of one who has his seat in the Munich Police Directorate, it gives one pause to think that people who would never put their own blood and skin on the line would instigate a development that would ultimately lead to a bloody confrontation.

It is also correct that there can be no understanding regarding South Tyrol with the real instigators of this Italy-bashing, as South Tyrol itself is just as indifferent to these elements as is German ethnicity in general. Rather, it is merely a suitable means for causing confusion and riling up public opinion, especially in Germany, against Italy. That's what matters to these gentlemen.

And the Italian objection, that no matter how the treatment of Germans in South Tyrol may be, these people would always find something suitable for their agitation because they want to, also has a certain justification. However, precisely because today in Germany, just as in Italy, certain elements have an interest in thwarting understanding between the two nations by all means, it would be a matter of prudence to deprive them of these means as much as possible, even at the risk that they would continue to seek them out. The opposite would only make sense if there were no one in Germany who had the courage to speak out for understanding against this agitation. But this is not the case.

On the contrary, the more today's Italy tries to avoid all unwise incidents, the easier it will be for Italy's friends in Germany to expose the agitators here, to reveal the hypocrisy of their reasons, and to put an end to their nation-poisoning activities. If, however, one truly believes in Italy that it is not possible to somehow accommodate the clamor and demands of foreign organizations, as this would resemble a capitulation and could possibly only increase the arrogance of these elements, then ways could be found to attribute such accommodation fundamentally to those who are not only not involved in this agitation but who, on the contrary, as friends of understanding between Italy and Germany, themselves wage the sharpest struggle against the poisoners of public opinion in Germany.

The foreign policy goal of the National Socialist movement has nothing to do with either economic or bourgeois border policies. Our national spatial goal will also in the future assign to the German people a development that will never need to lead it into conflict with Italy. We will also never sacrifice the blood of our people to bring about minor border adjustments but always only to gain space for further expansion and nourishment of our people.

This goal drives us eastward. What the Mediterranean Sea is for Italy, the eastern coast of the Baltic Sea is for Germany. Germany's mortal enemy for any further development, indeed even for the mere preservation of the unity of our Reich, is France, just as it is for Italy. The National Socialist movement will never fall into shallow external jingoism. It does not want to brandish the saber.

Its leaders have almost without exception experienced war as it truly is.

Therefore, it will never shed blood for other goals than those that serve the entire future development of our people. It therefore also rejects provoking a war with Italy for any other purpose than the alleviation of the spatial need of our people due to the ridiculous border correction in the face of German fragmentation in Europe.

On the contrary, it wants the unholy Germanic trek to the south to come to an end in the future and for the representation of our interests to take place in a direction that appears to our people to alleviate its spatial need. But by redeeming Germany from the period of its current enslavement and servitude, we are also fighting at the highest level for its restoration and thus in terms of German honor.

If today's Italy believes that a change in various measures in South Tyrol could be perceived as a capitulation to foreign interference without ultimately leading to the desired understanding, then it may make its adjustment solely for the sake of those in Germany who are themselves proponents of understanding with Italians and who not only vehemently reject being identified with the agitators but who have also fought the fiercest battle against these elements for years, and who recognize the sovereign rights of the Italian state as naturally existing. Just as it is not indifferent for Germany whether it gains Italy as a friend, it is equally not indifferent for Italy. Just as fascism has given the Italian people a new value, so too must the value of the German people for the future not be assessed according to its current manifestations, but according to the forces that it has so often demonstrated in its history and that it may perhaps demonstrate again tomorrow.

Just as the friendship of Italy is worth sacrificing for Germany, so too is the friendship of Germany equally valuable for Italy. It would be a blessing for both peoples if those forces could come to an understanding, which in both countries are proponents of this realization. As much as the agitation in Germany against Italy is to blame for the unfortunate enmity, so much blame also lies on Italy's side if, in the face of the fact that there is a fight against this agitation in Germany itself, it does not also proactively take the means out of their hands as far as possible. If the wisdom of the fascist regime manages one day to make 65 million Germans friends of Italy, then this is worth more than if one were to educate 200,000 into bad Italians.

Similarly, it was incorrect for Italy to advocate for a ban on the annexation of Austria to Germany. The fact alone that France primarily advocated for this ban should have led to the opposite position in Rome. Because France is not taking this step to benefit Italy, but rather in the hope of being able to inflict harm on it.

There are primarily two reasons that motivated France to push through the annexation ban: First, because it wishes to prevent the strengthening of Germany, and second, because it is convinced that one day it will maintain a link to the Austrian state as part of the Franco-European alliance. In Rome, one should not be deceived that French influence in Vienna is significantly more decisive than even the German one, not to mention the Italian.

The French attempt to relocate the League of Nations to Vienna only stems from the intention to strengthen the cosmopolitan character of this city and to relate it to the country whose essence and culture find a stronger resonance in the current Viennese atmosphere than the essence of the German Reich.

As serious as the annexation tendencies of the Austrian provinces are in themselves, they were taken lightly in Vienna. On the contrary, when Vienna truly operated with the idea of annexation, it was always to solve some financial difficulty, because then France was much more willing to come to the aid of the small pump state again. However, this annexation idea will gradually diminish to the extent that there is an internal consolidation of the Austrian Federation and Vienna regains its full dominant position. Additionally, the political development in Vienna is increasingly taking on an anti-Italian and particularly anti-fascist character, while Austro-Marxism has always made no secret of its strong sympathies for France.

Thus, the fact that the annexation was fortunately prevented at that time, partly with Italian help, will one day fit the missing link between Prague and Yugoslavia into the French alliance system.

Preventing the annexation of Austria to Germany was also wrong from a psychological perspective for Italy. The smaller the fragmented Austrian state remained, the more limited were naturally its foreign policy objectives. One cannot expect a state entity that has barely... sq km of land area with hardly... million inhabitants to have grandiose geopolitical ambitions. If German-Austria had been annexed to Germany in 1919/1920, the tendency of its political thinking would gradually have been determined by the great, if only possible, political goals of Germany, a nation of almost 70 million people. By preventing this at the time, the direction of foreign policy thinking was shifted away from larger goals and limited to small, old Austrian reconstruction ideas. Only in this way was it possible for the South Tyrol question to become significant at all.

Because as small as the Austrian state was in itself, it was still large enough to become the carrier of a foreign policy idea that corresponded as much to its smallness as it could slowly poison the political thinking of all Germany in turn. The more limited the political thoughts of the Austrian state will be due to its spatial limitation, the more they will eventually dissolve into problems that may have significance for this state but cannot be felt as decisive for the shaping of German foreign policy.

Italy would have to advocate for the annexation of Austria to Germany in order to thwart the French alliance system in Europe. Furthermore, it would also have to do this to present other tasks to the nucleus of German border policy due to its incorporation into a large empire. Moreover, the reasons that once prompted Italy to oppose the annexation are not quite apparent. Neither present-day Austria nor present-day Germany can currently be considered military adversaries for Italy.

However, if France succeeds in creating a general alliance against Italy in Europe, in which Austria and Germany participate, then the military situation will not change at all, whether Austria is independent or whether it is with Germany. Moreover, one cannot truly speak of the independence of such a small entity. Austria will always be tied to the strings of some great power. Switzerland cannot prove the possible opposite in the slightest, as it, as a state, albeit based on tourism, still has its own means of livelihood. This is impossible for Austria due to the discrepancy between the capital of this country and the size of the entire population. However, regardless of the stance Austria takes towards Italy, the fact of its existence already relieves the military-strategic situation of Czechoslovakia, which may one day become apparent in relation to Italy's natural ally, Hungary, in one way or another.

Military and political reasons would speak for the Italians to regard the annexation ban as at least meaningless, if not advisable.

(C) I cannot close this chapter without now specifically determining who is actually to blame for the existence of the South Tyrol question.

For us National Socialists, the decision has been made in terms of constitutional law, and at least I, who vehemently oppose dragging millions of Germans onto a battlefield and letting them bleed for France's interests without any resulting success for Germany that in any way corresponds to the blood sacrifices made, also refuse to recognize the standpoint of national honor as decisive here. Because, based on this perspective, I would still have to march against France first, which has violated German honor through its actions in a completely different way than Italy. I have already expressed my views on the possibility of making the concept of national honor the basis of foreign policy in the introduction of this book, so I do not need to address it further here. If our protest associations attempt to portray our stance as betrayal or abandonment of South Tyrol, then this could only be correct if without our stance South Tyrol would either not have been lost at all or would be on the verge of returning to the other Tyrol in the foreseeable future.

I am therefore compelled, in this statement, to precisely establish once again who betrayed South Tyrol and through whose measures it was lost for [Austria] Germany.

1. South Tyrol was betrayed and lost due to the actions of those parties that, through long years of peace, weakened or completely rejected the armament necessary for the assertion of the German people in Europe, thereby depriving the German people of the necessary power for victory in the critical hour, and thus also for the preservation of South Tyrol.

2. Those parties that, through long years of peace, undermined the moral and ethical foundations of our people and, above all, destroyed the belief in the right of self-defense.

3. South Tyrol was betrayed by those parties as well who, as so-called state-preserving and national parties, were indifferent or at least watched without serious resistance. They are, albeit indirectly, complicit in the weakening of our people's military strength.

4. South Tyrol was betrayed and lost due to the activities of those political parties that had degraded the German people to the agents of the Habsburg imperial idea. Instead of presenting the goal of national unity of our people as the aim of German foreign policy, they saw the preservation of the Austrian state as the task of the German nation. They watched for decades, even in peace, the deliberate de-Germanization efforts of the Habsburgs and even contributed to it, thus also being complicit in the failure to solve the Austrian question by Germany itself or at least with decisive German involvement. In such a case, South Tyrol would certainly have remained with the German people.

5. South Tyrol was lost due to the general lack of goals and planning in German foreign policy, which in 1914 also prevented the establishment of reasonable war aims or extended them.

6. South Tyrol was betrayed by all those who did not contribute to the utmost to strengthen German resistance and offensive capabilities during the war. Both through the parties that deliberately paralyzed German resistance and those who tolerated this paralysis.

7. South Tyrol was lost due to the inability, even in wartime, to reorient German foreign policy and to save the Germanic nature of the Austrian state by relinquishing the preservation of the Habsburg great power.

8. South Tyrol was lost and betrayed by the activities of those who, during the war, under the pretense of the hope for a peace without victory, broke the moral resistance of the German people and brought about a peace resolution that was fatal for Germany instead of a manifestation of the will to war.

9. South Tyrol was lost through the betrayal of those parties and men who, even during the war, lied to the German people about the

absence of imperialist goals of the Entente, thereby deceiving our people, alienating them from the absolute necessity of resistance, and ultimately making them believe the Entente more than their own warners.

10. South Tyrol was further lost through the weariness of the front caused by the homeland and through the contamination of German thinking with the dizzying declarations of Woodrow Wilson.

11. South Tyrol was betrayed and lost through the actions of the parties and men who, starting from draft dodging to the organization of the ammunition strike, robbed the army of the feeling of the unshakable necessity of its fight and its victory.

12. South Tyrol was betrayed and lost through the organization and execution of the November crime, as well as through the shameful and cowardly tolerance of this disgrace by the so-called state-preserving national forces.

13. South Tyrol was lost and betrayed through the shameless actions of the men and parties who besmirched the German honor after the collapse, destroyed the reputation of our people before the world, and thus only awakened the courage for the greatness of demands among our opponents. It was further lost through the pathetic cowardice of the national bourgeois parties and patriotic associations, who dishonorably capitulated everywhere before the terror of commonness and treachery.

14. South Tyrol was finally betrayed and lost through the signing of the peace treaties and thus through the legal recognition of the loss of this territory.

The blame for all of this lies with all German parties. Some deliberately and intentionally destroyed Germany, while others, in their proverbial incompetence and their cowardice that cries out to heaven, not only did nothing to stop the destroyers of the German future but, on the contrary, through the incompetence of their domestic and foreign leadership, they actually played into the hands of these enemies of our people. Never before has a people been destroyed by such a marriage of meanness, treachery, cowardice, and stupidity as the German people.

These days, insight into the activities and workings of this old Germany in foreign policy is provided by the publication of the war memoirs of the Chief of the American Intelligence Service, Mr. Flynn.

For a broader understanding, I will let a bourgeois-democratic organ speak:

(26th June 1928)

How America Entered the War

Flynn publishes from the diplomatic intelligence service - by F.W. Elven, representative of the Munich Neuesten Nachrichten - Cincinnati, mid-June

In the widely-read weekly magazine Liberty, William J. Flynn publishes a part of his war memoirs. Flynn was the head of intelligence for the United States during the war. This service covers the entire country and is brilliantly organized.

In times of peace, its main task is to provide personal protection to the President. It also takes care of anything else in the federal capital that needs or believes it needs protection. It monitors all doubtful elements suspected of having joined political movements directed against the state and its leaders.

During the war, its main task was to monitor those who had made themselves more or less loudly known as opponents of the war, or who were suspected of not agreeing with Wilson's war policy. Even the Germans enjoyed his special care, and many fell into the traps set everywhere by the federal intelligence service.

But from Flynn's memoirs, one learns that the intelligence service was already assigned an important task before our entry into the war. In 1915, two full years before the declaration of war, the most capable telephone expert was summoned to Washington and tasked with arranging the telephone wires leading to the German and Austrian embassies in such a way that officials of the intelligence service could eavesdrop on every conversation held by either side with the ambassadors and their staff, and every conversation originating from the embassy rooms. A room was set up where all the wires were ingeniously connected so that not a single conversation could be missed.

In this room, secret agents sat day and night, dictating the overheard conversations to the stenographers sitting next to them. Every evening, the head of the intelligence service, the author of the article in Liberty, received the stenographic record of all conversations held in the last 24 hours, enabling him to inform the State Department and President Wilson of all important matters that same evening.

Note the timing - it was at the beginning of 1915 when this arrangement was made, a time when the United States still lived in peace with Germany and Austria-Hungary, and Wilson never tired of assuring that he harbored no hostile intentions against Germany. It was also the time when the then-German ambassador in Washington, Count Bernstorff, never missed an opportunity to acknowledge Wilson's friendly attitude and friendly feelings toward Germany and the German people. Around the same time, Wilson instructed his confidant Baruch to slowly begin mobilizing industry for the war; a time when it became increasingly clear, as the American historian Harry Elmer Barnes points out in his book on the origins of the Great War, that Wilson was firmly determined to enter the war and only postponed the execution of his war plans because public opinion still had to be won over to these plans.

Flynn's publication must definitively undermine the foolish talk that Wilson was pushed into the war against his will by the German U-boat warfare. The tapping of the telephone wires leading to the German embassy was done with his knowledge. This, too, is revealed in Flynn's publication. The author adds that the material collected in this way against Germany contributed significantly to the eventual rupture.

This proves to me that this material provided Wilson with the means to win public opinion for the war he had long planned. And indeed, this material was perfectly suited for that purpose. The publication confirms in full what unfortunately has had to be said repeatedly, that Germany at that time was represented in Washington in an incredibly incompetent and incredibly undignified manner. When one hears that Flynn writes at one point that the stenographic reports prepared for him every day contained enough material to keep a divorce lawyer busy for months, one gets an approximate idea of what was going on.

The intelligence service maintained female confidants in Washington and New York who had to eavesdrop on members of the German embassy, including Bernstorff, when anything important was happening. One of these confidants had a better lodging in Washington, where the gentlemen met with their ladies, and where occasionally Secretary of State Lansing also came to hear the latest news. On New Year's Day 1916, when news of the sinking of the Persia had become known in the federal capital, Bernstorff called five ladies in turn to pay them sweet compliments and exchange similar compliments, even though there can hardly have been a lack of serious occupation because of the mood that the news of the Persia's sinking left behind in the State Department and the White House.

One of the ladies complimented Bernstorff, saying that he was great in love - a great lover - and always would be, even if he lived to be a hundred years old. The other gentlemen of the embassy were no different. One, whom Flynn describes as the best diplomatic force of the embassy, had a friend in New York, a married woman, with whom he had daily telephone conversations costing the German Reich $20 each time, and whom he visited frequently. He told her everything that was going on, and she then made sure it was put in the right places. Even quite ordinary remarks about Wilson and his wife were made in the telephone conversations, and one can easily imagine that this did not make the mood in the White House friendlier towards Germany.

How little was known about the country and its people in the German embassy, and with what childish plans they occupied themselves, is revealed in conversations that took place in early March 1916. At that time, a resolution introduced by Senator Gore was pending in Congress, urging the American people to refrain from using armed merchant ships. President Wilson fiercely opposed the resolution. He needed losses of American lives to whip up sentiment against Germany. In the German embassy, it was known that the prospects of the resolution were not favorable, so they seriously considered buying Congress.

They just didn't know where to get the money from at first. On March 3, the Senate decided to temporarily postpone Gore's motion. The vote in the House was to take place a few days later. So the plan to buy the House first was eagerly pursued, but in this case at least, Bernstorff was sensible enough to strongly advise against the plan.

The reading of Flynn's article must leave every person with healthy German blood in their veins with a feeling of bright outrage, not only about Wilson's treacherous policy, but also, and especially, about the incredible stupidity with which the German embassy played into this policy. Wilson entangled Bernstorff more and more every day. When Colonel House, his confidant, returned from his European trip in May 1916, Bernstorff traveled to New York to meet him there. However, Wilson, who had pretended to have no objections to this meeting with Bernstorff, secretly instructed House to avoid any involvement with the Count and to avoid him at all costs.

And so it happened. Bernstorff waited in vain in New York. Then he went to a nearby beach and had himself photographed in a very intimate position in a bathing costume with two female friends. The picture is inserted in Flynn's article. At that time, it fell into the hands of the Russian Ambassador Bakmateff, who had it enlarged and sent to London, where it was published by the newspapers with the caption "The Dignified Ambassador" and served the Allied propaganda admirably.

This is what the Munich Neuesten Nachrichten write today. However, the man who is characterized in this way was a typical representative of German foreign policy before the war, just as he is also the typical representative of the Republic's foreign policy. This individual, who in any other state would have been hanged by a state court, is the representative of Germany in the League of Nations in Geneva.

These individuals bear guilt and responsibility for the collapse of Germany and thus also for the loss of South Tyrol. And with them, the blame falls on all parties and men who either caused such conditions, covered them up, passively accepted them, or did not fight against them with the utmost severity.

But the men who today brazenly attempt to deceive the public once again and try to portray others as the guilty parties for the loss of South Tyrol must first be called to account individually for what they have done to preserve it.

For my part, I can proudly declare that since the time I became a man, I have stood for the strengthening of my people, fought in the war for 1 mm at the German front in the West for 4 1/2 years, and since its end have been fighting against the corrupt creatures to whom Germany owes this disaster. That I have not made any compromises with the traitors of the German fatherland since that time, neither domestically nor in foreign policy, but have continuously proclaimed their eventual destruction as the goal of my life's work and the task of the National Socialist movement.

I can bear the barking of the cowardly bourgeois curs as well as the patriotic agitators all the more calmly, as I know only too well the average cowardice of these infinitely contemptible entities. The reason for their clamor is that they also know me.

————— 19 —————

CHAPTER 16
Conclusion

————— 28 —————

As a National Socialist, I see Italy today as the first possible ally of Germany who can step out of the camp of the old coalition of enemies without this alliance meaning an immediate war for Germany, for which we would not be prepared.

This alliance, in my conviction, will be of equal benefit to Germany as to Italy. Even if its direct benefit were to cease at some point, it will never turn into a detriment as long as both nations represent their own national interests in the highest sense of the word. As long as Germany regards the preservation of the freedom and independence of our people as the supreme goal of its foreign policy and seeks to secure the prerequisites for daily life for this people, its foreign policy thinking will be determined by the spatial constraints of our people. And as long as we will not have any internal or external reason to become hostile to a state that does not in the least hinder us in this regard.

And as long as Italy wants to serve its real life interests as a truly national state, it will also have to adjust its political thinking and actions to the territorial expansion of Italy, obeying the same spatial constraints. The prouder and more independent the Italian people will be, the less will its development ever come into conflict with Germany.

The areas of interest of these two countries are so happily far apart that there are no natural points of friction.

A nationally conscious Germany and an equally proud Italy will one day be able to heal the wounds left by the World War in the spirit of their sincere mutual friendship based on shared interests. South Tyrol will thus have a high mission to fulfill in the service of both peoples. When the Italians and the Germans of this region, filled with the responsibility for their own ethnicity, recognize and understand the great tasks that Italy and Germany have to solve, the minor disputes of the day will recede in the face of the higher mission of building a bridge of sincere mutual understanding across the former border between Germany and Italy.

I know that this is just as impossible under the current governments in Germany as it would be under a non-fascist one in Italy. For the forces that determine German politics today do not wish for a German resurgence, but rather its destruction. They also desire the destruction of the present Italian fascist state and will therefore spare no effort to sink the two peoples into hatred and enmity. France will eagerly seize upon any such, even if only thoughtless, expression and use it to its own advantage.

Only a National Socialist Germany will find the way to a final understanding with a fascist Italy and finally eliminate the threat of war between the two peoples. For this old Europe has always been an area dominated by political systems, and it will not be otherwise at least for the foreseeable future. The general European democracy will either be replaced by a system of Jewish-Marxist Bolshevism, to which state after state succumbs, or by a system of free and unbound nation-states, which in the free play of forces will imprint their character on Europe according to the number and significance of their respective ethnic groups.

It is also not good for fascism to exist as an idea in Europe in isolation. Either the thought world from which it comes will be generalized, or Italy will once again succumb to the general idea of another Europe.

So, when one examines Germany's foreign policy possibilities more closely, in Europe there are indeed only two valuable potential allies for the future: Italy and England. The relationship between Italy and England itself is already good today and, for reasons I mentioned elsewhere, is unlikely to deteriorate in the near future. This has nothing to do with mutual sympathies but is primarily based on Italy's reasonable assessment of the actual balance of power. Both states share a dislike for France's boundless and unlimited hegemony in Europe. For Italy, because its most vital European interests are threatened, and for England, because an overwhelmingly powerful France in Europe can pose a new threat to England's already somewhat uncertain maritime and global domination.

That this common interest, even if only quietly, already applies to Spain and Hungary today is justified by Spain's aversion to French North African colonization activities and Hungary's enmity towards Yugoslavia, supported by France.

If Germany were to succeed in participating in a new coalition of states in Europe, which would either lead to a shift in the balance of power within the League of Nations itself or allow certain power factors to develop outside the League of Nations altogether, then the first internal political prerequisite for later active foreign policy activity could be fulfilled. The disarmament and thus practical defenselessness imposed on us by the Treaty of Versailles could, albeit slowly, come to an end. This is only possible if the former victorious coalition itself falls apart in this matter, never, however, whether in alliance with Russia or even in conjunction with other so-called oppressed nations, against the encircling common front of the former allied victor states.

In the distant future, perhaps a new association of nations can be envisioned, consisting of individual states of high national value, which could then counter the looming domination of the world by the American Union. For it seems to me that the existence of English world domination causes less suffering to today's nations than the emergence of an American one.

However, no Pan-Europe can be called upon to solve this problem, but only a Europe of free and independent nation-states, whose areas of interest are kept separate and clearly defined.

For Germany, the time can only come when, secured by a rebuffed France and supported by the reconstituted armed forces, it initiates the resolution of its spatial constraints. But once our people have grasped this great spatial-political goal in the East, not only clarity but also stability of German foreign policy will ensue, which will prevent political insanities for at least a foreseeable future, like those that entangled our people in the World War. And then, finally, the period of petty daily squabbling and completely unproductive economic and border policies will be overcome.

Therefore, Germany will also have to proceed internally to the strongest concentration of its resources. It will have to recognize that armies and navies are not built and organized according to romantic, but practical needs. It will then naturally emerge as our main task to form an overwhelmingly strong land army because our future lies not on the water but in Europe.

Only when the significance of this sentence has been fully recognized, and in the spirit of this realization, the spatial constraints of our people in the East have been generously ended, will the German economy cease to be a factor of world unrest that summons a thousand dangers upon us. It will then, at least in the major aspect, serve the satisfaction of our internal needs. A people that no longer needs to push its rural population as factory workers into the big cities but can settle them as free farmers on their own land will open up an internal market for German industry that can slowly withdraw and relieve it from the raging struggle and the scramble for the so-called place in the sun in the rest of the world.

Preparing for and eventually implementing this development is the foreign policy task of the National Socialist movement. It must, from its ideological perspective, also place foreign policy in the service of the reorganization of our people. Here, too, it must anchor the principle that one does not fight for systems but for a living people, that is, for flesh and blood that must be preserved, for whom daily bread must not be lacking so that, as a result of its physical health, it can also be mentally healthy.

Just as it must stride over a thousand resistances, misunderstandings, and malice in its domestic reform struggle, it will also have to clear up politically, both with the conscious treason of Marxism and with the mass of worthless, indeed harmful phrases and notions of our national, bourgeois world. The less understanding there is currently for the meaning of its struggle, the more tremendous will be its success in the end.

Why Italy today, first and foremost, can be considered as an ally for Germany, is related to the fact that in this country, and only in this country, both domestic and foreign policy are determined solely by Italian national interests. These Italian national interests, however, alone do not contradict German interests, and conversely, German interests do not run counter to them. And this is not only important for factual reasons but also for the following:

The war against Germany was led by an overpowering world coalition, in which only a part of the states could have a direct interest in the destruction of Germany. In many countries, the transition to war occurred due to influences that in no way arose from the real internal interests of these peoples or could benefit them in any way. Enormous war propaganda began to obscure the public opinion of these peoples and to inspire them for a war that could not bring any benefit to these peoples themselves, sometimes even contradicting their true interests.

The power that caused this tremendous war propaganda was international world Jewry. Because as senseless as the participation in the war might have been for some of these nations from the standpoint of their own interests, it was as sensible and logically correct from the perspective of the interests of world Jewry.

It is not my task here to provide a treatise on the Jewish question itself. This cannot be done within the framework of such a short and necessarily condensed presentation. However, for better understanding, the following should be said:

Judaism is a people with a racially not entirely homogeneous core, but nevertheless, as a people, it possesses particular essential characteristics that distinguish it from all other peoples living on Earth. Judaism is not a religious community, but the religious bond among Jews is actually the current constitutional form of the Jewish people. The Jew has never had a territorially delimited state of his own in the manner of Aryan states.

Nevertheless, his religious community is a real state because it ensures the preservation, multiplication, and future of the Jewish people. However, this is the task of the state alone. The fact that the Jewish state is not subject to territorial limitation, as is the case with Aryan states, is related to an aspect of the Jewish people's nature that lacks the productive forces necessary for the construction and maintenance of a territorial state.

Just as every people possess the instinct for self-preservation as the basic tendency of its entire earthly activity, so does Judaism. However, due to the fundamentally different disposition of Aryan peoples and Judaism, the struggle for life is also different in its forms. The foundation of Aryan life struggle is the land cultivated by it, which now provides the general basis for an economy that initially satisfies its own needs through the productive forces of its own people in the internal cycle.

The Jewish people, lacking their own productive capabilities, cannot carry out the construction of a territorially perceived state but need the work and creative activities of other nations as the basis for their own existence. The existence of the Jew himself thus becomes parasitic within the lives of other peoples. The ultimate goal of Jewish life struggle is the enslavement of productive nations. To achieve this goal, which has actually represented the struggle for existence of Judaism at all times, the Jew uses all weapons that correspond to the entire complex of his being.

Internally, he fights within individual nations first for equality and later for superiority. For this purpose, he uses qualities such as cunning, cleverness, deceit, trickery, and dissimulation, which are rooted in the essence of his ethnicity. They are stratagems in his struggle for survival, just as the stratagems of other peoples are in sword combat.

Externally, he tries to unsettle nations, divert them from their true interests, plunge them into mutual wars, and slowly elevate himself to their master through the power of money and propaganda.

His ultimate goal is the denationalization, the mixed breeding of other peoples, the lowering of the racial level of the highest, and the domination of this racial mixture by exterminating the national intelligentsia and replacing them with members of his own people.

The end of the Jewish world struggle will therefore always be bloody Bolshevization, which in truth means the destruction of the own intellectual upper classes associated with the peoples, so that he himself can ascend to the master of humanity made leaderless. Stupidity, cowardice, and wickedness work in his favor. In the bastards, he secures the first openings to penetrate a foreign national body.

The end of Jewish rule is always the decline of any culture and finally the madness of the Jew himself. For he is a parasite on nations, and his victory means as much the death of his victim as his own end. With the collapse of the ancient world, the Jews faced young, partially still completely unspoiled, racially instinctive nations that denied him entry. He was a stranger, and all lies and disguises helped him little for almost half a thousand years.

Only feudal rule and princely rule created a general condition that allowed him to join the struggle of a suppressed social stratum, indeed, to make it his own in a short time. With the French Revolution, he received civil equality. This now provided him with the bridge over which he could step to conquer political power within nations.

The 19th century gives him a dominant position within the economy of nations through the expansion of loan capital based on the interest idea. Through the detour of the share, he finally gained possession of a large part of the production facilities, and with the help of the stock exchange, he slowly becomes the ruler not only of public economic but finally also political life. He supports this rule through the intellectual degeneration of nations with the help of Freemasonry and through the work of the press that has become dependent on him.

In the newly emerging fourth estate of manual laborers, he discovers the possible power for the destruction of bourgeois intellectual rule, just as the bourgeoisie once was the means to smash feudal rule. Bourgeois stupidity and indecent moral depravity, greed, and cowardice work in his favor. He forms the profession of manual workers into a special class, which he now lets take up the fight against national intelligence.

Marxism becomes the intellectual father of the Bolshevik revolution. It is the weapon of terror that the Jew now applies ruthlessly and brutally. Around the turn of the century, the economic conquest of Europe by the Jew is almost complete, and he now begins with political security. This means that the first attempts to eradicate national intelligence are made in the form of revolutions. He takes advantage of the tension among the European peoples, which is largely due to their general lack of space, by deliberately inciting them to world war. The goal is the destruction of internally anti-Semitic Russia as well as the destruction of the German Reich, which still opposes resistance to the Jew in administration and army. Another goal is the overthrow of those dynasties to which a democracy dependent on and guided by the Jew had not yet been superior.

This Jewish objective has at least partially been completely achieved. Tsarism and Kaiserism in Germany were eliminated. With the help of the Bolshevik revolution, the Russian upper class and also Russian national intelligence were murdered and completely eradicated under inhuman tortures and cruelties.

The total victims of this Jewish struggle for dominance in Russia amounted to 28-30 million dead for the Russian people. This is 15 times more than the cost of the World War for Germany. After the successful revolution, he tore apart all bonds of order, morality, custom, etc., abolished marriage as a higher institution, and proclaimed instead general mating with each other with the aim of breeding a general inferior human mush through unregulated bastardization, which is inherently incapable of leadership and which the Jew ultimately cannot do without as the only intellectual element.

To what extent this has succeeded and to what extent natural reactionary forces may still bring about a change in this most terrible crime against humanity of all time will be taught by the future. At the moment, he is striving to bring the remaining states to the same state. He is supported in his efforts and actions and covered by the bourgeois national parties of the so-called national patriotic associations, while Marxism, democracy, and the so-called Christian Center appear as the offensive combat troops.

The most bitter struggle for the victory of Judaism is currently taking place in Germany. Here it is the National Socialist movement that has taken up the fight against this accursed crime against humanity. In all European states, a partly silent and fierce struggle for political power is currently being fought, even if often only under cover.

This fight is decided, initially apart from Russia, also in France. There, the Jew has formed a common interest with French national chauvinism, favored by a number of circumstances. Jewish finance and French bayonets have since become allies.

This fight is undecided in England. The Jewish invasion is still met there by an old British tradition. The instincts of Anglo-Saxonism are still so sharp and alive that one cannot speak of a complete victory of Judaism, but rather that it is still partly forced to adapt its own interests to the English. If the Jew wins in England, then English interests will fade into the background just as German ones are no longer decisive for Germany today but rather Jewish ones. If, on the other hand, the Briton triumphs, then a change in England's attitude towards Germany may still take place.

The struggle for dominance of Judaism is also decided in Italy. With the victory of Fascism, the Italian people have triumphed in Italy. Even if the Jew is forced to adapt to Fascism in Italy today, his attitude towards Fascism outside of Italy reveals his inner conception of it. Since the memorable day when the fascist legions marched into Rome, only its own national interest has been decisive and determining for the fate of Italy.

For this reason, no other state is as suitable as Italy today as an ally for Germany. It is only the bottomless stupidity and treacherous malice of our so-called Volkisch [nationalist] movement that they would reject the only state currently governed nationally and prefer to ally with the Jews in a world coalition as genuine German nationalists. It is fortunate that the time of these fools in Germany is over, and thus the concept of German nationalism is disentangled from the embrace of as many petty and miserable creatures. It will gain immeasurably as a result.